EXTINGUISH BURNOUT

A Practical Guide to Prevention and Recovery

EXTINGUISH BURNOUT

A Practical Guide to Prevention and Recovery

Robert Bogue and Terri Bogue

Society for Human Resource Management
Alexandria, Virginia I shrm.org

Society for Human Resource Management, India Office
Mumbai, India I shrmindia.org

Society for Human Resource Management
Haidian District Beijing, China I shrm.org/cn

Society for Human Resource Management, Middle East and Africa Office
Dubai, UAE I shrm.org/pages/mena.aspx

SHRM®
BETTER WORKPLACES
BETTER WORLD™

This publication is designed to provide accurate and authoritative information regarding the subject matter covered. It is sold with the understanding that neither the publisher nor the author is engaged in rendering legal or other professional service. If legal advice or other expert assistance is required, the services of a competent, licensed professional should be sought. The federal and state laws discussed in this book are subject to frequent revision and interpretation by amendments or judicial revisions that may significantly affect employer or employee rights and obligations. Readers are encouraged to seek legal counsel regarding specific policies and practices in their organizations.

This book is published by the Society for Human Resource Management (SHRM). The interpretations, conclusions, and recommendations in this book are those of the author and do not necessarily represent those of the publisher.

SHRM, the Society for Human Resource Management, creates better workplaces where employers and employees thrive together. As the voice of all things work, workers and the workplace, SHRM is the foremost expert, convener and thought leader on issues impacting today's evolving workplaces. With 300,000+ HR and business executive members in 165 countries, SHRM impacts the lives of more than 115 million workers and families globally. Learn more at SHRM.org and on Twitter @SHRM.

Library of Congress Cataloging-in-Publication Data

Names: Bogue, Robert, 1972- author. | Bogue, Terri, author.
Title: Extinguish burnout : a practical guide to prevention and recovery / Robert Bogue and Terri Bogue.
Description: First edition. | Alexandria, VA : Society for Human Resource Management, [2019] | Includes bibliographical references and index.
Identifiers: LCCN 2019012956 (print) | LCCN 2019015233 (ebook) |
    ISBN 9781586446352 (pdf) | ISBN 9781586446369 (ePub) |
    ISBN 9781586446376 (Mobi) | ISBN 9781586446345 (pbk. : alk. paper)
Subjects: LCSH: Burn out (Psychology) | Job stress.
Classification: LCC BF481 (ebook) | LCC BF481 .B64 2019 (print) | DDC 158.7/23—dc23

Printed in the United States of America

FIRST EDITION

PB Printing 10 9 8 7 6 5 4 3 2 1   61.19504

Dedication

We dedicate *Extinguish Burnout: A Practical Guide to Prevention and Recovery* to our families.

Terri didn't get the benefit of knowing her father, Fritz, for long, but he left her with a lasting connection. The stories and memories of Fritz fused into a guardian angel that she could depend on throughout her life, except when swinging on the monkey bars. Terri's mom, Carol, carried the burden of both parents and became Terri's biggest fan (until Rob came along). Carol showered Terri with unwavering love and imparted the belief that anything was possible. These beliefs empowered Terri to reach beyond her wildest dreams. Fritz and Carol provided a foundation based on love that has continued and spread beyond their lifespan.

Rob's father, also named Robert, left an indelible mark on his desire to both create and understand how things work. Rob's mother, Carrie, challenged and encouraged him. She cheered him on as he struggled to learn the true meaning of the lessons that both she and Robert had taught Rob. Beyond the biological truism of genetics, Rob owes much of what he is to them both.

Our history defines us, and so too do we seek to be strong examples for our children. Somehow, they've found ways to challenge us and create new adventures that force us to continue to grow and adapt. In this struggle, the children have taught us new skills to avoid burnout—or at least the need to develop new skills to avoid burnout. We are forever grateful to our children for their love and devotion. May this book provide each of you with tools to avoid burnout and live a life full of passion and joy.

Table of Contents

Introduction

This project started both as a direct result of our need for it and through a serendipitous nudge. With seven kids, three business lines, a patent that has been pending for two and a half years, and countless projects in various stages of stuck, we were struggling.

The news all around us was screaming out that we weren't alone. Though our circumstances were unique to us, the challenge of avoiding burnout wasn't. Gallup reports that only 33 percent of employees are engaged, and about 66 percent of full-time workers experience burnout on the job. Reports say that 78 percent of physicians are sometimes, often, or always burned out (Physicians Foundation 2018). The Institute for Healthcare Improvement goes so far to say that, if burnout in healthcare were described in clinical or public health terms, it might well be considered epidemic (Perlo et al. 2017).

ENGAGEMENT AND BURNOUT

Organizations today are facing incredibly low employee engagement scores. By grading standards, nearly every organization is failing. However, the path from disengaged to engaged employees isn't always clear. Certainly, the annual employee surveys have data that says employees aren't happy, but it's not completely clear how to address it. Better—and more—communication can help. Maybe putting free soda or snacks in the break room could help. Maybe the organization will have to put in a café—but will that solve the problem?

In many cases, it will make it better but not solve the disengagement problem. Employees are caught in disengagement because they're stuck in burnout. They're not disengaged with the organization, they're disengaged with their career—or with life. They've fallen into the trap of burnout.

> Burnout is a continuum, and we're all somewhere on the continuum. We'll teach you how to move towards less burnout and more engagement with life.

Burnout is the opposite end of the spectrum from engagement. People who are burned out are unable to be excited about their organization or what they're doing. It's simply not possible.

BURNOUT IS RECOVERABLE

The key to fixing engagement isn't a new vacation policy. The key is in removing burnout from everyone. The key is helping employees avoid and recover from burnout—whether the burnout comes from work, home, or the community. Burnout bleeds from one area of their life into another; even if it's not caused by work, the productivity impacts are felt there.

Burnout itself has been well diagnosed with the Maslach Burnout Inventory (MBI) and, more recently, the Copenhagen Burnout Inventory (CBI). However, diagnosis isn't a cure. That's what this book is about. Rather than offering a way to diagnose burnout, we offer a set of models and skills that make it possible for you to recover from burnout yourself.

Instead of labeling you as burned out, we'll explain how burnout is a continuum, and how we're all somewhere on the continuum. We'll teach you how to move toward less burnout and more engagement with life.

MODELS AND METHODS

As you work through this process, we explain two models of how burnout functions. The models are complementary models. The first model, which has been dubbed "the bathtub model," explains how burnout looks when you're investigating the present and the future. It focuses on what fills your personal agency—and what drains it. In this model, burnout happens when your personal agency bathtub is empty.

The second model, the "perception model," takes a past-focused approach. It focuses on how you perceive what results are reasonable and what you've achieved. The power of the model is in your ability to ground your perceptions in reality and to adjust them.

Collectively, you can see how the things that you are doing—or have done—and your expectations are driving the degree to which you're feeling burned out today and how likely you are to be burned out in the future.

The models form the basis of the discussion on recovery and resilience that comprises the final third of the book. The skills that you'll develop in the final third of the book work equally well whether you're recovering from burnout or looking to prevent it in yourself and others.

GET SHORTY

The chapters in the book are intentionally short. No chapter is more than about 2,500 words. That's the length of a long article. You should be able to read each chapter in four to six minutes. We knew that if you're struggling with burnout, you don't need to read for an hour before you feel like you accomplished something.

We want you to know that you are making progress. Even before you get to the resilience section, you'll start building the resilience you need by simply becoming aware of how burnout starts and grows in your life.

At the end of each chapter, we have included a few discussion questions. These questions are designed to help enhance the content with your own experience and life. These questions can be used individually or in a group setting. You may want to use a journal to write your responses or simply ponder them as you give the information in each chapter the chance to come to life in your mind. If you are a manager using the book with your employees, you might use these questions to facilitate discussions. We hope you use these questions to help on your journey to preventing or recovering from burnout.

FOR YOU AND YOUR FRIENDS

We wrote this book for us, for our friends, and for the people we interact with. This book is designed to be accessible for anyone who has struggled with burnout and anyone who works with or cares about others who may be struggling with burnout. We're particularly interested in those of you who are managers—in your ability to help others recover from burnout when you find them there and prevent burnout in employees who are free from its grips.

While much of what we've written here is research based, our intent is to make the content understandable, so that, no matter your background, you can make sense of it. If you're an expert in HR, this book will be an illumination of the path to burnout. If you're an employee, mother, father, wife, husband, daughter, son, or just some random human, you will be able to read and understand the book. The research notes are marked in the text if you seek a deeper understanding.

ACKNOWLEDGMENTS

It's difficult to explain what it's like to put together a book for those who haven't had the honor of doing so. The best that we can get is that it's like watching one of your children graduate. You recognize, in that moment, the immense amount of work that went into the accomplishment. As parents, you can certainly take a share of the credit for leading them to this important event in their lives. However, just as clearly, you realize that there are teachers, coaches, family members, and friends that have nudged, pushed, supported, and sometimes carried your child to help them reach this point.

Books are the same. We get to put our names on the author line but there are so many others whose work brought the book to life. First, we'd like to thank our office manager, Dana Lheureau, for her tireless efforts to clean up our language and manage the project to completion. The work simply wouldn't be nearly as good without her tireless efforts.

We'd like to thank our friend Arnel Reynon, who created the fabulous cover in the midst of a personal tragedy. We're honored to have such a talented friend who is willing to share their art with the world.

Some of the contributions are less visible. Johnna VanHoose Dinse did an amazing job of indexing the book. When you're looking for information beyond the flow of the chapters, you can easily find it thanks to her. We were pleased when an old friend introduced us to her—and more pleased when we saw the great work that she does.

Finally, the publishing team at SHRM demonstrated so much persistence in helping us make this book be the best it can be. It's great to get to work with such talented professionals.

CHAPTER 1

What Is Burnout?

Before speaking about how to prevent something or recover from it, one must first understand what the "it" is. When it comes to burnout, the answers as to what it is aren't easy to come by.

The classic definition of burnout is a feeling of being exhausted, cynicism, and a loss of personal effectiveness (Maslach 2011). While these may (or may not) be useful criteria for assessing whether someone has burnout or not, for most people, it isn't meaningful. It doesn't separate those with burnout from those without. The problem is that everyone has felt exhausted at some point in their life. Everyone has been cynical. Everyone has felt like they are not being effective. These feelings can be as familiar as an old friend, yet they can signal burnout or a point on the pathway toward burnout.

> The classic definition of burnout is a feeling of being exhausted, cynicism, and a loss of personal effectiveness.

Other approaches to defining burnout have focused on the belief that it's a mismatch between what an organization (of any sort) needs and what the person is able and willing to provide (Maslach and Leiter 1997). While this shifts the focus from the effects of burnout to potential causes and may be more helpful in trying to understand how to prevent and recover from burnout, it's still quite nebulous. Therefore, it does little to serve our purposes of figuring out what to do about it.

BURNED-OUT SHELL

If we go back into the first definition of burnout, the imagery is of a house that's been consumed by fire, with walls still standing. The structure itself remains, but everything inside is a charred ruin. In some cases, it may be that the damage is barely visible from the outside—perhaps some smoke char around the windows or in the soffits near the roof.

Visible or not, people who are experiencing burnout feel hollow. They know something feels amiss, but they're not sure what it is. Sometimes, to escape from the feeling, they work harder and try to do more. They will do almost anything to drown out the feelings of emptiness. No matter how hard they try to fill the gap with distractions or diversions, the hollow remains. The distractions can cover the void for a time, but sometimes these distractions add to the feeling of hollowness because they present just one more thing to do.

In some cases, the diversions become addictions. What was once a drink after a particularly hard day becomes two—and a drink or two on the days that aren't so bad either. Instead of the coping skill that allows someone to function under stressful and unusual circumstances, it becomes the only way to survive life. It's as if these coping skills are all that's left holding up the shell of the human.

PROGRESSIONS

Burnout leads to many places. While some who are experiencing burnout land in a world of an addiction—or several addictions—many others find themselves in different predicaments. Instead of an addiction that has a central focus, they find themselves stuck in the quagmire of depression. While burnout isn't officially recognized in DSM-5—the fifth edition of *The Diagnostic and Statistical Manual of Mental Disorders*—depression most certainly is (American Psychiatric Association 2013). Depression, in summary, is characterized by a sustained sad or depressed mood, an inability to feel joy, and, in some cases, activity retardation.

Also not recognized in DSM-5 is another disruptive state called "acedia." Acedia is a "lack of care." This may be a lack of caring for things that one once cared for or a general lack of drive. Acedia is a challenge. It was once recognized as an "evil thought" by monks as they struggled to articulate their malaise, but the condition fell out of popular awareness. When the monks' eight evil thoughts were eventually converted to the seven deadly sins, acedia was lumped in with sloth (Norris 2008). Today, the DSM-5 criteria for depression are so broad and inclusive that they sweep acedia up into the same general category.

Could it be that the continued rise of depression in our country isn't really depression as much as acedia, or that the cause of both may be an increased incidence of burnout raging through the country? Could it be that, despite the continued rise in general affluence, we find ourselves feeling more and more lost and alone? It could be that our affluence leads us to the belief that we don't need anyone else, and this prevents us from being connected in ways that help us resist falling into the trap of burnout.

LEARNED HELPLESSNESS

Rewind the clock a bit and position yourself in the lab of Martin Seligman. It's 1967, and there's a bunch of dogs in the lab receiving small shocks to test their responses. Some try to find a way to escape the shocks, and others don't even try. They lie down and whimper. Seligman and his colleagues described this as "learned helplessness," the feeling that nothing can change one's current state (Seligman and Maier 1976). The dogs who had given up trying to escape their shocks had learned, through previous experiences, that they couldn't escape the shocks, so they didn't even try.

Burnout convinces people that they're not able to change their circumstances, and therefore they shouldn't even try, or vice-versa. That is, people develop burnout because of their perception that they're unable to change their circumstances. Whether learned helplessness leads to burnout or burnout leads to learned helplessness, it's clear that they're correlated.

> Most people who are burned out have lost their connections with other human beings.

In the social human experience, most people who are burned out have lost their connections with other human beings. This is critical because, in our human experience, we know that those who care about us can sometimes lend a helping hand. That helping hand can be more than enough to change things—if it's the right person at the right time (Freudenberger and Richelson 1981). Knowing that others we're connected to have hidden capacities and resources that they may use to assist us keeps hope alive that things can really change for the better.

CONNECTEDNESS

We're wired to be connected. We're wired to be in relationships with other people. Jonathan Haidt describes our ability to "mind-read" others as the "Rubicon crossing" that changed our evolution. He believes that this ability was a clear defining line in our ability to work together and therefore tame the Earth (Haidt 2012). We are, as much as we prefer our individualism, social creatures who are meant to be in relationships with one another.

Our hectic world today makes us superficially more connected through the instant access of smart phones and a global internet, but we're three times more likely to report having no one to discuss important matters with, or connect with, than in 1985 (McPherson, Smith-Lovin, and Brashears 2006). Connections are powerful; loneliness has the capacity to alter DNA transcription in ways that increase the risk of inflammation-related diseases. Despite being more technically connected, we feel more alone (Cacioppo and Patrick 2008).

Technology is one of the driving forces that makes us more technically connected yet personally distant. We brag about how many Facebook friends we have, yet Americans say that they have fewer "real" friends than ever before (Turkle 2011).

DIMENSIONS

On the one hand, we experience burnout through our work or through difficulties at home; on the other, we realize that the patterns that cause burnout aren't confined neatly into one aspect of our lives. We may feel burnout toward work but come home to our families and feel relatively fine. It's equally likely that the emptiness that pervades burnout will spread like a fire to every aspect of our lives.

Burnout has a habit of sneaking up on us. It slowly convinces us that things will never change. It's the whisper in our ear that things will never get better, the tea leaves that seem to say we'll never achieve our goals, so we should just give up on them. Burnout slowly lowers us into learned helplessness.

Even if we recognize that we're burned out in one aspect of our lives, perhaps we're stuck in a job we hate until the kids get out of college and the demand for a high income is reduced. We may feel burned out and stuck in our jobs, but we console ourselves that at least our home life is OK.

> The burnout in one aspect of our lives starts to carry over into other areas of our lives.

However, we don't recognize the bids for connection from our spouse. Ultimately, missing these bids for connection moves us further away from the very support that we rely on (Gottman 2011). Instead of enjoying our time at home, we're stuck reliving the events of the day and the insanity of it all. In small and large ways, the burnout in one aspect of our lives starts to carry over into other areas of our lives.

Burnout becomes a vortex, sucking up progressively more and more energy from other areas of our lives. If we've got a ritual of personal refreshment, from meditating to playing golf, we'll find that we can do it less often, or we're too distracted to get the benefits from it, or what was once life-giving becomes another chore we have to complete. Our relationships at home never seem to give quite enough to support our need for connection, value, purpose, and progress. Even in our social lives, the evenings at the lodge, the church, or out with friends seems—over time—to be insufficient to fill the hole that staying in a job we hate has created.

THE PATH

The good news is that there is a path around burnout—and one back from burnout if you've already traveled there. The paths aren't well-marked, and they're not easy to travel. However, once traveled, you'll likely find that you'll never wander back into burnout again.

The purpose of this book is to mark the path and prepare you for the challenges that lie ahead. In doing so, it's our hope that you'll be able to understand burnout, see it coming, and know how to avoid it. On the surface, the guidance in the book is simple. Connect with people, be true to yourself, set realistic expectations, and recognize your value. However, the devil is in the details. How do you connect with people in meaningful ways? How do you become—or remain—true to yourself if you've never met your real self or you don't like who you believe your real self is?

That's why we've got a whole book to get to know one another.

CHAPTER SUMMARY

- Burnout can be hard to define. You can feel cynical, exhausted, or ineffective without experiencing burnout. It's also not helpful to hear that it's a mismatch between what your company needs and what you can do since it doesn't help us understand how to avoid it.

- People experiencing burnout often feel hollow, like the shell of a burned house.

- Some people fill their hollowness with addictions. What was once a coping skill becomes the crutch that holds the person up.

- The hollowness in others can drive them into a depressive state or acedia. Acedia is a "lack of care," though nowadays it often gets swept into the general category of depression.

- Burnout often convinces you that you can't change anything, so there's no reason to even try anymore. This is known as "learned helplessness."

- People need connections to others. Burnout can cause people to disconnect.

- Like a wildfire, when burnout starts in one area of your life, its effects tend to spread to the others.

DISCUSSION QUESTIONS

1. What leads you to believe that you are (or were) experiencing burnout?

2. How do you believe that your situation and circumstances can change for the better?

3. Who would you say you feel connected to, and how are you connected to them?

4. Burnout is sometimes described as feeling hollow, like a burned-out shell. How would you describe the feeling of being burned out?

CHAPTER 2

How Burnout Works

Whether you're personally experiencing burnout or you're simply scared by the reports of those close to you who have tried to explain it, we know that it's not a place anyone wants to be. Before we can discuss the strategies that will help you recover from it or avoid it in the first place, we've got to understand how burnout works.

Here is the framework of how burnout sneaks up on us and what it means. With a basic framework in hand, we can evaluate techniques for escaping its clutches.

WHENCE DOES IT COME?

As we discussed in the previous chapter, burnout is classically seen in three factors: exhaustion, cynicism, and lack of personal effectiveness. Of these three components for burnout, which are candidates to cause burnout? In other words, which came first: the proverbial chicken or the egg?

Teasing out causality is notoriously hard in research circles. Indicating correlation—that two things tend to occur together—is statistically straight-forward. However, causation requires the introduction of time as an isolating variable, and, given the constraints of research grants, that can be challenging.

However, much like the proofs that we all hated in our geometry class, we can evaluate each of the criteria to evaluate whether it's a reasonable candidate to cause the condition.

Exhausted

"Overworked" and "overwhelmed" describe many American families today. It's more difficult to find someone who doesn't describe themselves as over-worked and overwhelmed in their job, their personal life, or in general than it is to find someone who does. We've become obsessed with success, mate-rial objects, and the experiences we *simply must* provide for our kids to the point where we leave ourselves exhausted.

Strangely, however, many of the people who are the most overworked, overwhelmed, and physically exhausted can't be said to be suffering from burnout. People who work the hardest on their jobs, for their communities, and with their families aren't the ones that seem to be suffering. However, this does not mean that those who work hard cannot experience burnout.

Certainly, there are those examples of high-performing people who seem to hit a wall and burn out, but the incidence of this happening is incredibly low. We probably all know a few people who are burned out. However, this is a small number among the thousands of people that we know, from near-strangers to friends and family. If we apply this ratio to the people we know best, in whom we feel confident we would notice burnout, the rate of burnout is very low, particularly among those who are working hard. Hard work doesn't seem to correlate with burnout in most peoples' experiences.

If you think about it, in our own lives, the times we've worked the hardest are often those we find the most fulfilling. The times we've poured our heart and soul into that project to make it perfect or successful or amazing aren't when we've felt the worst; in most cases, it's when we have felt the best. It isn't the work that drives our feelings—it's the perception of results. So, while it is true that people who are burned out feel exhausted, it doesn't seem to follow that, if you're striving, challenging yourself, and pushing for more, you'll necessarily feel like you're all used up.

Cynicism

Look around. Of the people around you right now, or the people who you were last with, who are the cynics? Are the cynics the young people, whether they are the newest workers at the office, the Starbucks server, or your children? Are they older people who have battle scars from long-forgotten battles, both imagined and real?

Cynicism arrives when people are let down. It happens when expectations of their lives, other people, or the world in general aren't met. Cynics accept the belief that there is no way to change the world, so it's okay to just complain about it.

Cynicism represents a clue to burnout since it is formed by the belief that nothing can ever change. It's having reached the stage of learned helplessness where you believe nothing you can do could possibly change the world or your corner of it. If you can't change things, how personally effective are you?

Perceived Personal Efficacy

> It's easy to see why the lack of perceived personal effectiveness may be the start of burnout.

In the light of cynicism and the idea that nothing you can do will make things different, it's easy to see why the lack of perceived personal effectiveness may be the start of burnout. Before it has reached its full development, where nothing is possible any longer, burnout starts as the feeling of not doing enough.

At the most basic level, the engine that drives burnout is the feeling and belief that you're not making progress toward your goal—even when you don't know what the goal really is. It's a simple statement, but unpacking it isn't easy. Even if we call it "perceived personal efficacy," in these three words there is a challenge.

Our perceptions are notoriously fickle things. There are a host of psychological biases that prevent us from seeing the world as it is. Biases like "what you see is all there is" may be a holdover from our pre-toddler days, but they haunt us still (Kahneman 2011). Our eyes may capture images of the world around us, but our brains construct the world around us from incomplete information provided by our limited view and often make up the answers when the answers aren't forthcoming (Eagleman 2011). As a result, we must know that our perceptions are not reality. The way we perceive the world is necessarily incomplete. This can be due, in part, to the fact that our perceptions view only one side of a world composed of multiple aspects. To address perception, we are led down the road of psychology, neurology, and, occasionally, ancient wisdom.

Personal is our second word, and it should be easy. After all, we've lived with ourselves our entire lives. No one should know more about us than ourselves. In one sense, this is absolutely true. We are the authority on our experience (Miller and Rollnick 2013). However, in another sense, there is so much about us that we don't know and don't realize. When we measure ourselves, what yardstick do we use? How do we account for our capacity to work with others to get things done? These questions and others make it hard to pinpoint where our personal capacity should end and another's begin.

Efficacy is a loaded word. In it is the idea that something is effective. Effective for what and at what scale? A spoon is effective at moving dirt when you're planting a tiny cactus in a terrarium. A spoon is completely ineffective when trying to build a road. Efficacy relies on context. In the case of humans, we establish what we want to get accomplished and work toward those goals.

In the word efficacy, we must consider how reasonable our expectations of effectiveness are and whether we have defined the right measurements to indicate progress.

PERSONAL AGENCY

Our belief that we're personally able to change our world, that we have control of our results in life, is a deep-seated belief that some might call a delusion. It allows us to proceed through our days without the fear that we'll be wiped out by an asteroid tomorrow. Belief in our personal agency needs to find a place in the middle between powerless and omnipotent. We need to find an understanding of what we can and cannot do.

In one view of burnout, you believe that your personal agency is depleted, that somehow you have given all you have, and there's nothing left to give. Personal agency is our actual ability to get things done, though this may be vastly different from our perception of this ability. It's both a measure of the time available to do things as well as our physical and emotional ability to get things done. Consider a man with a shovel and lots of time. He has the personal agency to move a mountain—or, at least, a hill of dirt. Similarly, a man with a backhoe and a bit less time can move the same hill. Personal agency is the ability to move the hill of dirt, whether with a shovel or a backhoe.

Figure 2.1 shows a simplified model of our capacity for personal agency, which we call the "bathtub model." Our personal agency, the bathtub, is filled by some activities, like water flowing from the tap, and reduced by others, like the drain pulling water out. Our ability to preserve our personal agency, to keep our bathtub full, is what keeps us from burnout.

> There are three sources that pour into personal agency: results, support, and self-care. The demands placed upon us decrease our reservoir of personal agency.

In this model, there are three sources that pour into personal agency: results, support, and self-care. The demands placed on us decrease our

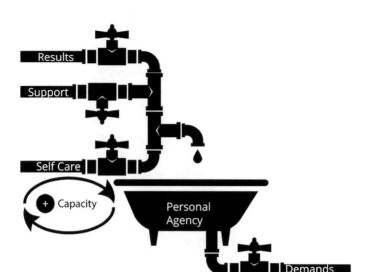

Figure 2.1. The simplified view of personal agency

reservoir of personal agency. Let's look at each of the components of this model and how they impact our ability to perceive that we have personal agency.

Results

If you want to perceive that you're effective—that you have personal agency—the easiest way to get that is to see results. A farmer can see the harvest from the seeds they planted and come to know that they have power over the Earth. A machinist can see the part they created. However, for the most part, our ability to see results is mitigated by the fact that our degree of influence is low, while the impact of the outside world is great.

Farmers must accept that the weather plays a substantial role in their ability to produce a bountiful crop. They see the results of their labor and know they can produce something, but the final volume of what they produce isn't entirely based on what they've done. As we move from tangible to intangible creations, it becomes harder to measure our results and connect how they have been influenced by us.

In many situations, we may influence the results but find it difficult to identify our impact. Because we can't see those results directly, it becomes harder to fill our personal agency with results.

Support

Despite the rugged, individualistic perspective of our world, we cannot escape the reality that we're all dependent on other human beings for our lives today. We're far removed from the days when we were truly self-sufficient—if those days ever existed. For most of us, we couldn't live without electricity and running water. Most of us don't know how to get water safely and heat our homes on our own.

Even in frontier days, families traveled together in a wagon train helping each other. More importantly, the community that formed in the wagon train helped each other and "circled the wagons" to protect the families from the dangers of those outside the community.

Once we've accepted that we are reliant on support from others, we can recognize that this support makes us stronger and gives us the ability to do great things. Sir Isaac Newton said, "If I have seen further it is by standing on the shoulders of giants." It is from this point of view that we can say we gain more personal agency when we are able to rely on others for support.

Let's take a simple example. Let's say that you have a yard that takes an hour per week of maintenance in the summer. If you care for the yard yourself, you'll invest twenty hours or so per year in caring for it. However, if you have a child who can take care of it, you have twenty hours of additional time available. That increases your personal agency by twenty hours.

On a more emotional and less concrete level, having someone who is there to listen and attempt to understand your day—such as a spouse or significant other—can be a source of strength and support and will help you be more able to provide this kind of support for others.

Self-Care

One of the most overlooked and often under-invested activities in anyone's life is self-care. Self-care is what you do for yourself to restore yourself and build additional capacity for personal agency. Not only does self-care fill you up, it changes your ability to be filled up. In a sense, it makes a bigger bathtub.

A trap that many seem to fall in is deferring self-care while serving the needs and demands of others. This is particularly true of those who are in caring roles. Pastors and nurses feel like their parishioners and patients need them more than they need to take care of themselves. However, like compound interest, investments in yourself make it possible for you to give more to others. You simply cannot give what you do not have, and if you don't take the time to rest and recharge, there will be nothing for you to give to others.

Self-care is necessary in the short and medium terms but has a longer and more powerful effect of increasing your capacity for personal agency. By developing a habit of self-care, you demonstrate your self-compassion and thereby create a greater capacity for personal agency.

Demands

Everyone has demands made upon them. From the routine electric bill to the extraordinary support demanded by your best friend in a time of need, demands on our abilities are a part of the human condition. Managing our reservoir for personal agency is as much about limiting the way we respond to the demands placed on us as it is about ensuring a steady supply of resources to replenish ourselves.

Often, the demands placed on us are unreasonable—or rather the way we want to respond to the demands is unreasonable. Certainly, if you have a best friend who needs you to take them to the airport you should—unless it represents a substantial sacrifice for you and means a relatively small benefit to them. We sometimes fail to test to see whether the demands that are being placed upon us personally, socially, and occupationally are reasonable.

Many who have a compassionate heart attempt to alleviate the suffering of others with no concern about how this depletes their own resources or reduces their own capacity to help others. We must recognize that we have a finite personal agency, and because of that, we can't afford to invest too much in everyone.

Consider a scenario where you're a medic on a battlefield. There are injured soldiers all around you, and some of them are going to die. It's not within your capacity to save them all. Training kicks in and you're suddenly in triage mode. You're trying to figure out how to save the most lives you can. You accept that zero fatalities is not an option, and you move to providing the greatest good and accepting the inevitable losses. All our demands in life are like this. To decide for one thing necessarily deprives us of another.

If we go watch a friend sing, we can't go to another's piano recital. If we choose to get ahead in our career, we'll necessarily make choices that lead us away from friends, family, and leisure.

Managing the demands that are placed upon us is perhaps the most difficult part of maintaining our personal agency and avoiding burnout.

> Managing the demands that are placed upon us is perhaps the most difficult part of maintaining our personal agency and avoiding burnout.

With these basic explanations and the functioning framework out of the way, let's take a deeper look into the three sources that fill up personal agency and the demands that draw from it.

CHAPTER SUMMARY

- Classically speaking, burnout has been described as feeling exhausted, cynical, or personally ineffective. However, it may be more useful to consider it in terms of personal agency.
- Personal agency is your actual ability to do something, though it might differ greatly from how we perceive this ability.
- In the bathtub model of burnout, there are three sources that pour into our personal agency: results, support, and self-care. The demands placed on us by ourselves or others act as a drain on our reservoir of personal agency.
- Results can help us perceive our effectiveness and personal agency accurately. By leaning on the support of others, we can gain more personal agency that we might have alone. Self-care not only refills your personal agency, but it can help you increase your capacity for personal agency, too.
- Managing the demands placed on us is probably the most difficult challenge in avoiding and recovering from burnout.

DISCUSSION QUESTIONS

1. When have you found yourself feeling like you have given all you have to give?

2. Think about two situations into which you poured all your energy: one that left you feeling energized, and one that left you feeling burned out. What was the difference?
3. What are some things you do that fill your personal agency capacity?
4. What are some demands that drain your personal agency capacity?

Perceived Results

Of the ways that fill your personal agency "bathtub," results are the most direct way of seeing that you're making a difference, thereby influencing your perception that you can have impact. It fills your personal agency reservoir quickly. However, the challenge is in how you perceive the results that you encounter. Do you perceive them as larger than they are or smaller than they are? Additionally, how do you cut through all the noise to see the trend in whether you're getting more or fewer results than you have in the past?

LARGER THAN LIFE

It was a crushing blow. The patient had just "fired" Sue, her nurse, and Sue was devastated. The patient was difficult, and Sue knew it, but she prided herself on taking good care of all her patients. She followed the rules and knew what it would take for the patient to get better. The patient was recovering from surgery, and though she didn't feel good, it was important that she brush her teeth. Sue insisted, and that's when she was "fired," and another nurse took over.

In truth, trouble had been brewing throughout the day. The patient didn't want to get up to go to the bathroom, and Sue had made her. Sue knew the research and knew that her patient needed to both get up and brush her teeth. More than that, Sue had received several awards initiated by other patients for her compassion and friendliness. However, being fired felt like a ton of bricks were just dumped on her.

At that moment, she was the worst nurse in the world who couldn't even keep from getting fired by a patient. As luck would have it, Jane, Sue's older and wiser friend from another unit, had come down with some paperwork. Jane knew about Sue's dedication to patients and the awards that she had received. Finding Sue in the breakroom, crying and trying to put herself back together, Jane sat down and began to listen.

Sue explained how she was a horrible nurse. Only bad nurses get fired from their patients. Only nurses who didn't make the cut were fired. This meant that Sue was one of the bad nurses. After letting Sue get it all out, including how hurt she was and how she didn't feel like she could do the job, Jane calmly stated that she had been "fired" from patients numerous times.

Sue couldn't hold back her surprise, and the tears stopped for a moment. "Really?" she asked in an unmistakably confused voice. Sue thought that Jane could do no wrong. Jane was the kind of nurse that Sue hoped she'd become someday. Jane was confident, effective, and compassionate.

Jane explained that being fired didn't mean that she was a bad nurse. Sometimes it was a bad personality match with the patient. Sometimes, like in Sue's case, she had to do the right thing for the patient—even if they didn't like it. Something started to click with Sue as she asked, "So, it doesn't mean I'm a bad nurse?"

Jane quickly had Sue review her awards and the feedback she received from her managers, doctors, and other nurses. Nothing pointed to Sue's being a bad nurse. Instead, it pointed to her being a very good, young nurse who was a great asset to her patients and to the organization. As Jane got up to go back to her unit, she offered her typical sage advice. "Things will look better in the morning," she said, and with that, she was gone.

Sue fell into the trap that thinking the result she was seeing—being fired—was the only result. She thought that every patient wanted to fire her, and that she was a bad nurse because of it. She had taken one incident and made it much larger than it really was. When she began to look at all the feedback she received, she realized that she was really making more of it than she should. She hadn't slept well the night before, so perhaps Jane was right: it would all look better in the morning.

> Sue fell into the trap that thinking the result she was seeing—being fired—was the only result.

SMALLER THAN REALITY

Tim had just won a big account. It was, in fact, larger than any account the firm had ever won. It was a monumental coup over a fierce competitor, and it was something that management was talking about for months after the sale. However, to Tim, it was just another client. You win some, and you lose some, he'd always say. He'd been in sales long enough to know that you'd lose more deals than you'd win, and he had convinced himself that winning this deal was no big deal.

It would single-handedly account for 25 percent of the firm's revenue within the first year, and everyone knew it, but still Tim wanted more. He got a good commission check, but by that time, he had lost two deals that he thought were in the bag. He began to be conscious of his losses and he failed to recognize that the firm's numbers were still substantially up because of his work on the big sale.

He didn't realize how his sales approach had been particularly insightful and that this was what sealed the deal for the client. Nor did he realize that his ability to articulate the value of his organization had changed and made their fiercest competitor just an also-ran, just another horse in the back of the pack with no real hope of winning the race.

> Tim didn't feel like he was any better at sales than a year ago—despite the straightforward evidence to the contrary.

The result was that Tim didn't feel like he was any better at sales than a year ago—despite the straightforward evidence to the contrary. Tim couldn't see a realistic perspective of the value that he had delivered to the organization or the results of his hard work. As a result, he felt like he couldn't continue to add value to the organization. Instead of seeing the results as too large, he saw them smaller than they really were.

THE IMPACT OF TIME

Jane's advice to Sue was right on multiple levels. Getting sleep is a powerful self-care technique, and it tends to help adjust perspective. It allows you to see things in the broader context of time. The immediate emotion you feel fades over time. Often, you realize that it's not all that bad. Perhaps another patient tells Sue that she appreciates the extra attention. Perhaps Sue gets the chance to see her niece and play a game of *Candyland*. Giving something time helps to put it into a better perspective.

If you can learn how to view time as a friend that will always be there with you, you can lean on time's perspective on whatever the current situation is. Looking forward in time, you can see that whatever it is that you're struggling with won't matter in the grand scheme of the universe. Looking back, you can frequently find that you would have been amazed to have the opportunity to have this sort of problem a few years ago.

It's what they call "first-world problems." We still have problems, and they feel incredibly important. But if you look back to your grandparent's generation, the challenges they faced were often more life and death.

That's not to say that your problems can't be present and challenging, but time can reduce their impact to a more balanced place. Both the setbacks that you encounter and the successes that you find can find their place in time.

With an understanding of how results—and your perception of results—pour into your personal agency bathtub, it's time to look at how support can improve your capacity to get things done, too.

CHAPTER SUMMARY

- Results are a fast way to fill your reservoir of personal agency.
- However, sometimes the way we perceive these results is either too large or too small.
- In Sue's case, she perceived her result—being fired from a patient—as being larger than it really was. She believed that now all her patients wanted to fire her and that she was a bad nurse because of it.
- In Tim's case, he made his results of winning the big account smaller than they were. Despite helping the organization tremendously and having a great overall year, he saw it as "just another sale."
- To help to see your results in the right perspective, it helps to lean on self-care in the form of sleep and rest; the positive support of others, like friends and family; and just a little bit of time.

DISCUSSION QUESTIONS

1. When was a time that you got a result, and you perceived it as larger than it really was?
2. Think about a time that others thought your actions or accomplishments were more amazing than you did. How did their perceptions change yours?
3. Think about an event at least ten years ago that seemed life-changing. Looking back at the event, how do you perceive its impact on your life today?

CHAPTER 4

Support

The most important support is support that is felt. You can't be filled up by something that you can't recognize. It's one thing to believe that you have others who care for you and support you; it's quite another to see this actually happen and be able to truly feel the support.

It's important to realize the many forms that support can take. For some, emotional support from family will be completely lacking. For others, it will be material support. Everyone has a collection of support systems around them that allows them to increase their personal agency. Here, we'll systematically review the types of support, the duration of the support, and the areas of support.

TYPES OF SUPPORT

Your personal agency may express itself in your ability to listen to others' pain and show them compassion. It may be a special skill that allows you to help others. It might be your financial resources. Or it may be your ability to build support systems around people that allow them to be successful. Similarly, the kinds of support that you can experience from others falls into categories of emotional, material, or systemic.

Emotional

There are many dimensions of how to provide emotional support. *How to Be an Adult in Relationships* (Richo 2010) presents a five-part framework, called the "Five *As*," that summarizes it well:

- **Attention**—Consciousness of the other person and their needs.
- **Acceptance**—Accepting the other person's reality as theirs, even if we don't agree.
- **Appreciation**—An attitude of gratitude for the other person.
- **Affection**—Demonstrating love for others (in whatever way they can receive it).
- **Allowing**—Permitting the other person to live their life without our attempts to control.

When people give us these things, they demonstrate their love and concern for us in ways that strengthen our resolve, so we're capable of meeting and overcoming the obstacles that we face.

It's important to take a moment and explain that, in this book, we'll use the English word "love" to refer to concern for our fellow man. The best Greek equivalent is the word *agape*. Occasionally, we'll speak of our love of our community or family, and we'll mean the equivalent of the Greek word *philos*. Where we use it, we'll refer to love of our community or family to make the meaning clear. It's important to realize that we aren't speaking of romantic or erotic love (which is the Greek word *eros*). It's unfortunate that the English language doesn't distinguish between these different kinds of love.

Though we can receive emotional support through our romantic partner, the love we're talking about is founded on our connection with any other human at an emotional level.

We'll spend a great deal of time in this book explaining various kinds of emotional support, since it's the most critical in preventing and recovering from burnout.

> We'll spend a great deal of time in this book explaining various kinds of emotional support, since it's the most critical in preventing and recovering from burnout.

Material

Not having the tools and resources that you need to do a job well can be intensely frustrating. You feel like you could do the work if you only had the right support. For some, materialistic support can be as little as someone cosigning a loan for your first "beater" car to get you to a job. For others, it's the support necessary to get through college with minimal debt. While material support is frequently seen as financial support, there are many kinds of material support that don't express themselves as money.

A spouse can agree to take on more of the chores at home. Grandparents can agree to watch their grandchildren to give their own children a break. There are innumerable ways that people can provide some tangible or material support to help fill up someone else's personal agency. One of the things that we see most frequently is when someone volunteers their skills to help someone else.

Rob's father is very mechanically inclined. He helps Rob's brothers in their business by repairing vehicles and equipment when they break in addition to driving trucks and helping run equipment. These kinds of material support make it possible for them to focus their attentions on other areas of the business that need their attention.

For us, we materially support our children by assuring them they'll always have food to eat and a place to stay. This allows them to take risks because they know they'll always have food and shelter. This is the real way that material support enhances your personal capacity. It's not just that you literally can get more done—it's equally important to realize that it allows you to take risks that you couldn't realistically take without that support.

Systemic

It seems like emotional and material support would be all there is. Either you're supporting mental health, or you're doing something tangible. However, there's a spot that exists for people to support you in ways that directly provide neither material nor emotional support. Instead, it's possible that you'll be supported by systems that make it easier for you to be successful. The welfare and unemployment systems in the United States are examples of systems that are designed to catch people who fall, therefore allowing for more risks. However, more important are those systemic factors that lead to the right results. They're like guard rails that make it possible for people to keep on the road instead of ending up off a cliff.

Systemic support may show up in governmental systems that prevent failure. It may show up in work systems that are designed to help managers be successful. Things like mentoring and buddy systems implemented at a corporate level are a kind of support that is systemic in nature. These systems reinforce changes for personal success, increasing the sense of personal agency.

DURATION OF SUPPORT

The support that you receive can be limited in time or it can be more diffuse and continuous. Episodic support might be the visit from a friend who isn't normally available, and continuous support may be in the form of loving parents or long-term friends who are generally always available to respond to a need.

With episodic support, you may find your personal agency increases. You may, for instance, feel more capable of climbing a mountain with a friend who is an avid mountain climber. Continuous support, in general, makes you more willing to explore your world and express your true self to others (Tough 2012).

When evaluating your personal agency, it's important to recognize that there are times when you will have more support—and therefore more personal agency—and times when you will have fewer resources supporting you.

AREAS OF SUPPORT

For each of us, there are areas where we feel more supported and places where we feel less supported. Here we will pause for a moment to review ways that you may be receiving support that you're not aware of or aren't connecting well.

Home

A wise friend once told me, "Happy wife, happy life." I'm not quite sure that it rises to the level of an ancient proverb, but I'm sure that it's been said before. Most of us find that, whether we're married or not, stability and strength in our home life allows us to extend more fully into the world.

It seems odd that we'd look to rats to teach us about how humans venture out into the world. However, researchers discovered that rat pups whose mothers gave them more licks and other grooming had different neural development. The behaviors of the mother literally changed how the young pups' brains formed. More important to our conversation is the fact that these pups were less fearful and more able to explore their environments (Caldji et al. 1998).

While there's a substantial amount of research that much of how a person develops is genetically influenced, there are also documented cases where nongenetic drivers can create risks and opportunities for people as they grow. For instance, prenatal stress in a mother can radically change how the brain of her child forms (Wood 2013).

> Our support at home is critical to our ability to experience our personal agency.

With the research indicating that our home lives and our family of origin can literally shape the forming of our bodies, it's not surprising that our support at home is critical to our personal agency. However, what may be surprising is that it's not just our parents that can help us experience our personal agency.

Alzheimer's is a debilitating disease that steals our memories from us. Debate continues as to the real cause. The two markers of the disease, extracellular plaques and intracellular tau structures, both seem to be implicated, but no one can definitively say what sets of the cascade of events that rips people from themselves. In some patients, fear sets in as they recognize that they're losing themselves bit by bit. Such was the case of Robertson McQuilkin's wife, Muriel. Muriel had stood beside Robertson as he was a missionary in Japan and served for half a century before becoming the president of Columbia International University. Robertson left his post to care for Muriel because she was agitated whenever he wasn't present. McQuilkin spoke of his decision: "This was no grim duty to which I stoically resigned, however. It was only fair. She had, after all, cared for me for almost four decades with marvelous devotion; now it was my turn." In three sentences, he summarized the power of a supportive spouse who allowed him to reach further by her presence and support in his life (Smith 2017; P. Miller 2009).

Siblings can be a substantial source of support as well. Consider what travel would be like today if it hadn't been for two brothers with a bike shop in Dayton who spent their winters with wind tunnels and their summers in a place called Kitty Hawk, NC. Orville and Wilbur Wright did what others could not by making human-powered flight possible. Even well-funded researchers like Samuel Langley couldn't beat the Wright brothers into the air. Their internal passion and their support for one another created massive personal agency for the brothers.

Children require a great deal of work. Parents make massive investments in their children, both materially and emotionally. However, sometimes our children provide support to us as well. Watching them grow can fill a parent with hope. Adult children can help their parents in material ways as well by fixing a car, a computer, a house, or a special meal. So, while there's no doubt that children can be a source of demands for material and emotional resources, they can also be a source of support.

Social

Families are spread out more today than at any other time in history. We and our families venture more frequently from our historical roots—and to places much farther away. While our families are a source of support, their distance can sometimes limit their ability to support us. However, even in times when families were more closely located, sources of support came from the social network around us as well. Friends, associations, and associates have always provided support, both emotionally and materially.

Old friends can provide support through their ability to help improve perspective. Being an old friend means that they've had the benefit of being with you for a long time. As a result, they can help you put things in their proper perspective. Friends can also help you connect with others who may be able to provide the right kind of material support. Whether it's a referral to a physician, attorney, or accountant, friends offer support by connecting you to their friends so that you find the right people who can provide material support—or at least limit the drain on resources by providing you with the material goods and services you need at the highest quality for the lowest cost.

> Old friends can provide support through their ability to help improve perspective.

When it comes to churches and associations, the news isn't good. We're not joining associations, clubs, and churches as we once did (Putnam 2000; Dickerson 2013; Barna Group 2014). Despite this reality, the groups that we are a part of can be a large source of support—particularly in their capacity to help us feel connected with other human beings.

In our new "gig economy," the support we receive from our colleagues and associates at work is changing. The line between what we do for work and how we socialize blurs as we move from project to project and group to group. However, most social support from work associates tends to evaporate as you move to the next job or project, so we'll address support—including social support—from those that you work with from the perspective of work support.

Work

Many believe that the highest calling of a leader is to be a servant to those that follow them (Greenleaf 1977). While not every manager could be called a leader, there are managers who lead by ensuring that the people who work for them are properly equipped to be successful in their role. Managers who provide support for their subordinates can provide a gentle ear and required resources. In doing so, they make it possible for their subordinates to be more powerful.

Conversely, subordinates are counseled to work in ways that help their manager look good. Whether or not subordinates subscribe to this ideal or not, they do increase your capacity to get things done. With good subordinates, you're able to get more done. Their ability to work with you to accomplish goals increases your personal agency.

Coworkers often have slightly different temperaments and skills from those you have. It could be that some love organizing the supply closet and others know how to make things fit into incredibly small spaces, while you find both kinds of work infuriating. When coworkers are a team and can share work in ways that play to everyone's strengths, it increases your ability to get things done.

Personal

The last—and perhaps most important—area of support is the support that you give yourself. No one else can take this kind of support away from you. But what is self-support? It comes in the form of self-care. It comes from recognizing your strengths and building your capacities. That's the subject of the next chapter.

CHAPTER SUMMARY

- There are three major types of external support: emotional, material, and systemic.
- Emotional support comes in many different ways. One model involves offering attention, acceptance, appreciation, affection, and allowing.
- Material support doesn't always mean financial support. It can also mean providing food or shelter or offering up your time for others.
- Systemic support often comes in the form of social services like government aid, but you may see it in the form of training or mentorship at work.
- It can be helpful to accept that there will be some times in your life with more support and some times with less. Just remember that support comes from various areas, such as from home, your social circle, and work, at various times.

DISCUSSION QUESTIONS

1. Think of at least three people who provide you support and what kind of support they provide. Who provides emotional, material, and systemic support, and how do they provide it?
2. What kind of support do you find is the most difficult to accept you're receiving?
3. Thinking back to when you were growing up, when did you receive support that you didn't recognize as support at the time?

CHAPTER 5

Material Self-Care

Self-care is at the heart of preventing and recovering from burnout. Self-care is the one thing in the burnout system that you truly have control over. If you are cognizant of your need to replenish yourself, you can perform the self-care you need to meet nearly any level of demand that might be placed on you.

In this chapter, we'll focus on the types of strategies for self-care. This chapter talks about the physical, or material, actions you can take to replenish yourself. Our next two chapters will focus on the psychological side of self-care and how to be comfortable with yourself.

STRATEGIES FOR SELF-CARE

It's easy to dismiss self-care as unnecessary or unimportant. It's equally easy to dismiss self-care as something more easily done in a distant monastery where people only need to chant endlessly for no apparent purpose. However, the truth is that most self-care is inherently practical. As we review some of the areas where you can express self-care, a more common issue isn't that the ideas aren't practical, but rather that we believe we're not worthy of the time spent on self-care. Others' needs are more important, we'll tell ourselves. We can get by without it for just a few days. The problem is that these are lies.

Perspective

> You get more personal agency—and additional capacity—through self-care. By depriving yourself of self-care, you're depriving others.

Before discussing the practicalities of self-care, we need to shift our perceptions to realize that we simply cannot give what we don't have. Let that sink in for a moment. If you don't have any personal agency left, you can't help others. You get more personal agency—and additional capacity—through self-care. By depriving yourself of self-care, you're depriving others.

For some who struggle with shame and lack of worthiness, it can be hard to accept the need to do things to support ourselves so that we can support others. It feels like we have an obligation to take care of others' needs before our own. Mothers believe that they should provide for their children before they take time to re-energize themselves. However well-intended this perspective is, it leaves us vulnerable to burnout as we run out of our personal agency.

Even those who are good at self-care can run into danger when they're willing to sacrifice their self-care for others day after day. It's appropriate to forgo self-care when a crisis emerges. However, evaluating what is truly a crisis for us and what is someone else's crisis is difficult. Just because someone else is having a crisis doesn't mean it's yours to fix. Sometimes they need to get themselves out of their own messes. Finding ways to get self-care back when it has been disrupted can be difficult.

So, while it's appropriate to sacrifice self-care for short periods of time, we must be on guard for when those sacrifices last longer than a day or two and we begin skipping self-care as a pattern.

PHYSICAL SELF-CARE

The relationship between how we feel emotionally and how we feel physically is well established (Pressman, Jenkins, and Moskowitz 2019). When we eat well, exercise, and generally take care of ourselves, we have a more positive outlook on life and build

> When we eat well, exercise, and generally take care of ourselves, we have a more positive outlook on life.

resistance against falling into the burnout trap. Physical self-care can come in the form of exercise, diet, sleep, and hydration.

Physical Exercise

There are those for whom physical exercise is an enjoyable experience that is its own reward. It's not like that for others. For some, physical exercise is a price that we must pay to be healthy and feel better. The impact exercise has on physical health is well documented. The impact of physical exercise on mental states is also found consistently in research. Physical exercise is related to significant improvements in mood and reductions in confusion, anger, and tension (Penedo and Dahn 2005). Whether it's something as simple as a walk or an aerobic exercise, physical exercise contributes both to your long-term health and to your emotional well-being.

It's not that you must join a gym and start on a bodybuilding career. Twenty to thirty minutes of moderate-intensity exercise on most days of the week is sufficient to experience positive impact (Penedo and Dahn 2005). Small, simple, and sustainable changes can increase your physical activity and reduce your chance of entering burnout (Deutschman 2009).

Diet

Dieting and nutrition are big business. There is no doubt that we've got a surplus of calories in our world today. The cheap abundance of high-calorie, low-nutrition, and highly palatable food has made obesity an epidemic in the United States and other countries. Food is your body's fuel. Putting the right fuel into it will make it run better.

The guidance on calories couldn't be clearer—don't eat more than the calories you expend. However, the other guidance becomes more nuanced. Some will recommend a low-fat diet, while others will advocate a low-carbohydrate diet. There are a few general guidelines that are agreed upon that can help you feel better:

1. **Don't eat empty calories**—Largely, this refers to sugar, but even starches and other foods that convert quickly to sugar should be limited. Diabetes is the disease that results when our bodies are no longer able to manage blood glucose (sugar) levels. Eating sugars and carbohydrates makes our blood sugar climb as our digestive system quickly absorbs and passes them along.
2. **Eat protein**—Our bodies are made of proteins, and we need proteins to be healthy. For many, this means meats and dairy products, but for our vegan friends, there are alternatives like quinoa and soy that provide protein without having to ingest meat or dairy.
3. **Vegetables and vitamins**—Just as we need proteins to be healthy, we need vitamins. The best way to get them is to eat fruits and vegetables that are rich in vitamins. Though vitamin supplements can help, they don't really take the place of a diet that includes fruits and vegetables.
4. **Finding fiber**—To help regulate our bowels, we also need to find ways of taking in enough fiber to support their healthy operation.

Sure, there's much more to managing your diet than these simple guidelines, but just by aiming toward these four things, you'll find that your body will have the fuel it needs.

Sleep

Sleep is critical to our health, both mentally and physically. Emotional regulation, for instance, is impaired when sleep quality is impaired (Mauss, Troy, and LeBourgeois 2013). Positive affect (mood)

> Research supports that poor sleep quality and burnout are correlated.

of adolescents is also negatively impacted by the lack of quality sleep (van Zundert et al. 2015). Research supports that poor sleep quality and burnout are correlated (Giorgi et al. 2018). Despite the awareness of the importance of sleep, Americans' nightly sleep has fallen from 9 hours in 1910 to fewer than 6.8 hours in 2013 (US Department of Health and Human Services, National Institutes of Health 2011; Jones 2013).

Making time and an environment for sleep can help your overall mood and reduce the impacts of burnout. Here are some helpful tips:

1. **Establish a sleep schedule**—Our bodies do not adapt well to changes in sleep schedule. Shift work disorder is a recognized form of circadian rhythm sleep-wake disorders caused by variation in sleep schedule (American Psychiatric Association 2013). The more you can keep to a regular sleep-wake cycle on both weekdays and weekends, the higher quality sleep you'll get.

2. **Your bed is for sleep**—By limiting the activities in bed to sleep and not prolonged periods of media consumption, we "train" our bodies to expect sleep when arriving in bed, resulting in a lower rate of insomnia and a shorter time to fall asleep.

3. **Limit electronics immediately before bed**—We live in an electronic world, but the light emitted from the screens contains a balanced spectrum of light, including blue light, that our bodies equate with daytime. Our melatonin production is low in the presence of blue light. When wavelengths of blue light are removed—such as would naturally happen around sunset—we develop more melatonin and a greater desire to sleep. Limiting electronics for thirty minutes preceding bed time can help some people.

If you're interested in tweaking your sleep to get better quality, there are several commercially available sleep monitors that can help you identify when you're sleeping well and when you're not. Over time, you can correlate what things you did that produced better sleep—and the things that produced interruptions to good sleep patterns.

Hydration

The positive effects of proper hydration can't be overstated. The body is 50–60 percent water, and maintaining that balance has impacts on our temperature regulation, physical performance, cognitive performance, and performance of the digestive, kidney, and circulatory systems (Popkin, D'Anci, and Rosenberg 2010). Even modest levels of dehydration can result in increased fatigue and headaches. Some research even demonstrates that mild dehydration leads to decreases in cognitive function, including decision-making and reaction time (Maughan 2003).

Here are a few key tips for keeping hydrated:

1. **Eighty-four ounces is a start**—The human body loses an average of eighty-four ounces of water a day through breathing and urinating. Plan to replace it.
2. **Strenuous exertion and high temperatures increase water loss**— If you're planning on any high-temperature activity, plan for additional water intake.
3. **Not all drinks are equal**—Drinks that contain caffeine, like soda and coffee, and alcohol are diuretics, which cause more water loss through urination. Plan on drinking more water if you drink any of these.
4. **Urine color is a validated way to assess hydration status**—Look for urine color scales like the US Army scale linked here (https://gacc. nifc.gov/nwcc/content/pdfs/safety/DOD_Urine%20Color%20Test_ Poster.pdf) and use your urination to monitor your hydration during the day. Take action if you find that you're dehydrated.

Physical self-care, while not always given its proper priority, is a necessary step in maintaining your personal agency. In the next two chapters we'll look at how psychological self-care is as essential as physical self-care.

CHAPTER SUMMARY

- Self-care is the things you do to replenish yourself. While some people neglect self-care, it's important to know that you can't help others if you don't help yourself first.
- Physical self-care often comes in four forms: exercise, diet, sleep, and hydration.
- You don't need to be a bodybuilder or marathon runner to see benefits from exercise. Even walking or doing yoga for twenty to thirty minutes a day can greatly contribute to your physical and mental health.
- Diets are simply what you eat. By limiting nutrient-poor foods, prioritizing proteins and nutrient-rich foods, and making sure to take in enough fiber, you'll find your physical body has the support it needs.
- Keeping a consistent sleep schedule, using your bed only for sleep, and limiting blue-light electronics before bed can help you sleep better and wake feeling more rested and refreshed.
- Water is crucial to your body's proper functioning. Generally speaking, drink more of it (at least eighty-four ounces every day). If you're in a hot climate, doing strenuous work, or drinking caffeinated or alcoholic beverages, drink even more. You can do a self-check to review hydration levels—lighter-color urine normally indicates better hydration.

DISCUSSION QUESTIONS

1. What do you do to practice self-care each week?
2. What circumstances lead you to minimize your self-care?
3. What are some ways you can improve your physical self-care?
4. What physical self-care activities do you find most enjoyable?

CHAPTER 6

Psychological Self-Care

S trangely, it is often easier for folks to practice physical self-care than psychological self-care. Part of this may be the stigma of mental health challenges and the desire to avoid getting wrapped up in activities that might have caused someone to look down upon them in their parents' or grandparents' generation. As the stigma associated with mental health issues slowly fades, the resistance will as well—but not necessarily fast enough to allow people to take up regular practices of psychological self-care on their own. That's why it's important to be intentional about how we take care of ourselves psychologically.

Burnout is a psychological concern. It doesn't mean a weakness; it is a mismatch between the situations that someone finds themselves in and their skills. Much like you wouldn't be expected to jump into the cockpit of a helicopter and start flying without training and support, you should not expect that you can handle every situation without training and guidance.

In this chapter, we'll focus our attention to the voices inside our head and to ways that we can rejuvenate ourselves while deferring the topic of coping strategies, addiction, and stress to the next chapter.

SELF-TALK

Have you heard the way that you talk to yourself? It sounds silly, but most people don't think about how they speak about themselves—to themselves. Do the voices inside your head tell you that you're smart? Funny? Worthy? Loved? Or are the voices inside your head telling you that you're worthless? A burden? Unlovable?

The greatest challenge to psychological self-care is to change the way that you talk to yourself. Somewhere along the line, you've internalized external voices and have made them yours. Whether it was a teacher, father, mother, or friend, somehow their voice got stuck in your head. The result was that you treat this voice—with whatever judgment, condemnation, or other baggage that was attached—as your voice. Because it seems to be your voice, it seems to be true.

The problem is that most of us don't speak to ourselves with the same level of care, compassion, and concern that we'd use with another human being. We condemn our actions and berate ourselves for the smallest of infractions.

One of the most powerful approaches to psycho-therapy is called cognitive behavioral therapy (CBT). CBT teaches people to think—self-talk—different-ly. However, just because it's a psychotherapeutic approach doesn't mean that you must enter counsel-ing to use it. While counseling may be appropriate for some, it's not always necessary.

> The problem is that most of us don't speak to ourselves with the same level of care, compassion, and concern that we'd use with another human being.

While we'll cover some of the techniques for changing your self-talk, there are numerous other tools and resources including books dedicated to helping you change your thinking. *Redirect: The Surprising New Science of Psychological Change,* for instance, shows readers how to think differently (Wilson 2011). *Hardwiring Happiness: The New Brain Science of Contentment, Calm, and Confidence* focuses on how to remove neg-ative patterns of thinking and emphasize positive thought patterns (Hanson 2013). These are just two of literally hundreds of books that are available to help you change your pattern of thinking—and self-talk—to ways that are friendlier and compassionate. Before we leave this section, let's look at some specific risks of self-talk and some techniques for changing yours.

Globalization and Personalization

Everyone receives bad news and disappointing feedback. We don't get select-ed for the team or event. We hear that we made mistakes. In short, we're not perfect. It's a good thing that we get the feedback. However, it stops being so good when we make that feedback global and personal.

Globalization of feedback is taking something from an instant of time, like "I swung and missed," and saying that it happens all the time—"I always miss." While, certainly, this can reflect the feeling of the moment, rarely is this true. It would be possible to tell Thomas Edison that he always failed at making lightbulbs—right until he succeeded. We don't know "always" or "never," because that would require us to see into the future, which we—obviously—can't do.

Often when we globalize things, we know, intellectually, that it's not true. Maybe just last week you hit the ball out of the park, but you're blinded to that reality after your missed swing. The problem with globalization is that it is almost never true. There are always exceptions despite the way that we sometimes talk to ourselves.

Personalization is another way that we can shape our experiences in a way that's not fair to ourselves. Personalization makes the fact that you weren't selected for the team a personal fault instead of a bad fit for the situation. We say "I missed because I'm bad" instead of saying "That was a good pitch." Instead of recognizing that there are times when we can do a good job, we're focused on the one time (or few times) when we weren't successful. We need to recognize that the situation has an impact on the outcome just like we do.

Even in disappointment, we don't own all the outcome. Some of it is based on the other parties involved, and some is based on the environment or structure of the system. More times than not, decisions aren't made about us as a person and are instead made for reasons that have nothing to do with us. When our self-talk makes it about us, it's more than likely not true.

Awareness that the Self-Talk is Happening

Sometimes the challenge is that we don't even realize that the self-talk is happening. It's been years now, but Rob was once working on a clinical study trying to prove that standards and information technology could improve the care of patients with diabetes (Clark et al. 2001). The results were impressive, but the startling thing was the realization that someone who couldn't "feel" their blood sugar was at high risk of having adverse events. Why? Because if you aren't aware there's a problem, you can't correct for it before it becomes an issue. The same can be said about our self-talk. If we can't recognize that the voices inside our head are talking, we have little hope of quieting them.

Even if you can't "hear" the voices in your head in the moment, taking the time at the end of the day to assess what you were hearing can be helpful because it's easier to detect that there was negative self-talk going on today than it is to detect it in the moment. If you're having trouble hearing the way you're talking to yourself, make a habit of end-of-the-day reviews. Over time, by doing this you'll develop the ability to hear the self-talk in the moment.

Adding Voices

Another way to be able to hear the voices is to intentionally add some self-talk. We can add some voices of trusted friends and mentors who we know always have our best interests at heart. We can ask, "What would they say about this situation or about me?" Walking through these hypothetical answers often causes the other voices already in your head—your existing self-talk—to start being louder. If the existing voices aren't aligned with what the people who care for you most would say, a conflict will erupt. However, this is the right kind of fight to have in your head.

Fighting with Facts

By now, you may already be picking up on the idea that we're fighting the feelings and the self-talk with the facts. Not every self-talk conversation can be changed by focusing on facts, but a surprising number of them can. Many of the stories that we tell ourselves are just that—stories. When we examine the facts objectively, we see that we are making a difference, that we do have value, that we are enough, and that we're OK.

The people who care about you the most are likely to remind you of the facts. If those voices aren't loud enough, confront your self-talk with what you know to be the truth about yourself. Don't say to yourself, "I'm a good person." Respond with the good things that you've done. While our self-talk might argue whether you're a good person or not, it can't argue that you took dinner to a friend from church last week—that's a historical fact.

> Many of the stories that we tell ourselves are just that—stories.

Lying with Labels

Sometimes in our youth we're told that we are something. Not that we're good at something or that we've done good work—that we *are* something. The problem with this is that we get stuck in the identity. Instead of being able to accept that the label is a part of who we are, it becomes a core and immutable part of the identity that we seek to show to the rest of the world.

Carol Dweck has done a great deal of research into the mindsets that we can find ourselves in and how to encourage growth mindsets in others. Her book *Mindset* explains that fixed mindsets box people into a way of thinking that is either limiting, if you're capable of more, or frustrating, if you miss your expectations for that thinking (Dweck 2006). A growth mindset says that we're always growing and getting better, and just because we've failed today doesn't mean that we'll fail tomorrow.

Changing our self-talk to accept that we're still a work in progress makes it easier to accept our setbacks and to develop hope in our future capacity.

INTEGRATING YOUR SELF-IMAGE

Much of the challenge with negative self-talk comes from a lack of integration in our self-image. In some ways, we see ourselves as part of the universe, and in others, we see ourselves as unworthy of the love we receive from others. Pulling together these various views and getting to one appropriate, humble perspective can be challenging but rewarding. In fact, Richard Lazarus explains in *Emotion and Adaptation* that our ability to understand ourselves more completely changes the way that we appraise situations and how we feel about them (Lazarus 1991).

The process starts by recognizing the boundaries of what you will and what you won't do. (We discuss boundaries in greater detail in Chapter 8: Demands.) The clearer you can become on who you are, the less your self-talk can be negative. It's harder for the self-talk to speak negative lies when the truth about who you are is easy to see.

Once you've defined who you are through your boundaries, it's possible to move forward into accepting yourself as you are. In acceptance, you can respond to the self-talk differently. Instead of worrying about whether you're a flawed human or not (you are, and so are we), you can accept that you have flaws and will make mistakes and are just doing the best you can to be the best person you can be.

The best person you can be is someone that accepts who you are today and is willing to grow tomorrow.

REJUVENATING ACTIONS

Actions in the context of psychology seems like an oxymoron. How can thought be action? The answer is in our behaviors. One of the ways that we care for ourselves is aligning our behaviors to our thoughts and beliefs. The old saying "The road to hell is paved with good intentions" doesn't mean that our good intentions are bad—it simply acknowledges the potential for a gap between thinking (our intentions) and doing.

Simply doing what we say we're going to do relieves a great deal of psychological stress in the difference between the person we say that we are—who we believe ourselves to be—and our own observations of our behaviors. We can say that we value family and want to visit our aunts and uncles; but as another year rolls around, and we didn't get to see them, we must adjust our perception, change our behavior, or justify the "temporary" discrepancy.

Some of the actions that we can take are more than just aligned to our thinking; they're rejuvenating. For instance, someone who enjoys learning may find that reading or taking a class rejuvenates them. The specific topic of the learning is often secondary to the act of learning itself. Others may be problem-solvers who love solving puzzles, either as games or as tangible problems. We have a solar-powered minibarn, for instance, because there was a problem to be solved in getting power from our house a few hundred feet away to the minibarn. It wasn't a burden but was instead a way to rejuvenate and reinvigorate. It's not what is being done but how we approach and interpret what we're doing.

If you don't know what actions are rejuvenating for you, a psychological profiling test may help. Tools like Gallup's CliftonStrengths (Rath 2007), the Myers-Briggs Type Indicator, the DISC, and the Enneagram (Riso and Hudson 1996) attempt to sort your personality into categories. These tests are publicly available in both consumer and professional versions and typically come with reports and supporting materials that help you understand the kinds of activities that give you energy. The examples in the preceding paragraph used CliftonStrengths terms and associated activities, but they could have just as easily referenced another profiling tool.

Caution should be exercised to not read too much into these tests and their results, as no personality characteristics are good or bad. Sometimes people believe that being introverted—or extroverted—is a bad character trait, or they perceive that others look down on them because they have a particular character trait. Instead of looking for good or bad, look for opportunities

> Instead of looking for good or bad, look for opportunities to better understand yourself.

to better understand yourself. These tests can be a useful tool to direct your search for activities that rejuvenate (Paul 2004).

CHAPTER SUMMARY

- One of the greatest challenges to psychological self-care is the way we talk to ourselves.
- We all have voices in our heads. They might sound like our own voice but are often the words of parents, teachers, or others. In these voices, we are frequently more critical of ourselves than we would ever be to any other person.
- It can be easy to globalize an event, to believe you always do something wrong or you are never successful. These globalizations are not based on truth. The futures of "always" and "never" do not exist.
- Once you become aware of what the voices in your head are telling you, you can begin to fight these feelings with facts. Compare what you hear with what you see and what people you trust tell you.
- Learning who you are and what your boundaries are is an important step in developing an integrated self-image. From this point, you can begin to accept your flaws and recognize your strengths.
- Rejuvenating actions are those activities that support the person we strive to be.
- Multiple profiling tests are available that can help you find the kinds of activities that rejuvenate you. Remember these tests are only tools to help you better understand yourself; they do not define who you are.

DISCUSSION QUESTIONS

1. What do the voices in your head say to you? How do their stories match what your friends, family, and coworkers say about you?
2. What activity do you do that rejuvenates you? If you cannot think of one, what activity would you find rejuvenating that you might be able to participate in?
3. Think about a recent situation when the voices inside your head condemned or berated you. Compare this with the evidence that you saw around you and the reality of the situation. How could you have talked to yourself with more compassion?

CHAPTER 7

Psychological Self-Harm Prevention

Psychological self-care is a critical part of preventing or recovering from burnout. Psychological self-care can go wrong in so many ways that it's important to evaluate both the positive aspects of psychological self-care as well as how some of our self-care strategies may lead us astray.

We'll look at how our coping strategies form the foundation of our psychological protection mechanisms, and how we can develop addictions when they fail. We'll close with a discussion on how we manage stress and how stress management is good self-care.

COPING STRATEGIES

Some of the things that we do, such as eating sweets, release neurochemicals that help us feel better. Other things we do can similarly reduce our stress and improve our psychological well-being. These activities are called "coping strategies." Whether they have a recognized and accepted neurochemical basis or not, they help us feel better. Long-term, sustained stress has a variety of negative effects on our physiology and psychology (Sapolsky 2004). Choosing healthy strategies that reduce our stress and protect our health is important.

Healthy strategies for coping are called "adaptive" strategies. "Maladaptive" strategies have a higher likelihood to fall into abuse. A few strategies that are generally considered adaptive are:

- **Petting pets**—Our domesticated pets have been bred for their usefulness to humans. In our modern world, the usefulness is often emotional support. Petting a puppy, snuggling a snake, or clinging to a cat can be a source of stress relief—for both you and the pet (Kis et al. 2017).
- **Catching comedy**—Comedy is a built-in safety mechanism for predictive failures and releases a set of neurochemicals that can reduce the appearance of stress (Hurley, Dennett, and Adams 2011).
- **Connecting with conversations**—Conversations with other people—that don't relive negative incidents—can be powerful ways to reduce stress by providing assurance that you're not alone. This can happen by showing up to a local hangout or by making a specific effort to meet and connect with someone.

- **Selecting service**—Serving others helps to get you outside of yourself, reducing your stress and providing context that you're not alone in your struggles.
- **Having hobbies**—Hobbies can be intrinsically fulfilling and help reduce the stress in other areas of your life. This presumes that it is an established hobby that you find enjoyment in. Finding a new hobby when you are stressed isn't the best time.

In addition to the adaptive coping strategies above, there are some strategies that can be adaptive or maladaptive based on how they're used. For instance, eating is required for life, thus eating a relaxing, well-prepared meal may be an adaptive strategy when used occasionally. However, overeating and lack of compensating exercise leads to being overweight and its own set of health problems.

Compartmentalization is a necessary coping strategy that allows us to temporarily defer our full processing of a situation until the situation has reached its conclusion. This may be because it's necessary to focus on the use of professional skills instead of processing the emotion of an event. Consider a situation where you're a doctor, and your father collapses from an apparent heart attack. There's a fear for your father, the potential loss, and your own mortality to consider—but at a more appropriate time. In the moment, you need to use your medical training to try to save his life. Compartmentalization becomes bad when you never come back to process the event.

> You can—and should—use compartmentalization when appropriate for short periods of time while recognizing that the longer you use it, the more progressive damage you're doing.

Years ago, video cassette recorders introduced the ability to pause a video. You could stop at any spot you wanted. While you were paused, a tape-read head continuously rotated over a single section of the tape. If you left the recorder paused on the same place long enough, you would break the tape. As a result, most VCRs wouldn't allow you to stay paused on the same spot for very long. Compartmentalization is like this process. You can—and should—use compartmentalization when appropriate for short periods of time while recognizing that the longer you use it, the more progressive damage you're doing.

Rob's grandmother passed away around noon on his second day of a two-day engagement in Manhattan. He had work that needed to be completed to help the client launch their new program. He received the news, took a few minutes to compose himself, then compartmentalized it away until he could get on the plane to come back home and be with family. That compartmentalization was adaptive—but only because he came home and processed his emotions.

Coping strategies can reduce stress and provide enjoyment as well as connection, but ensuring coping strategies remain adaptive can be complicated at times. Sex can be a coping strategy that has a positive psychological and physical impact and provides intimacy within a stable relationship. Sex can be maladaptive if the pursuit of sex is compulsive or dangerous. When a coping strategy moves from being an optional choice for a safe behavior to something that must be done or is dangerous, it has become an addiction.

THE ROAD TO ADDICTION

Addictions are bad (Hari 2015). However, addictions aren't just for recreational drugs. Addictions come in the form of overeating, gambling, sexual activities, narcotics, alcohol, and many, many more. Addictions are a situation where a normal coping strategy progressively takes more control over the individual in increasingly harmful ways until the individual becomes powerless against the addiction.

That's why screening for an addiction sometimes revolves around whether the activities are unnecessarily dangerous or are compulsory. If you have control of your coping strategy, then it's not compulsory—and you don't do it when it's dangerous.

Obviously, there are caveats to this. For instance, skydiving might be a hobby that you enjoy. At some level it's dangerous—but it's also not likely to be an addiction unless you start to steal to support the fees to be able to jump. (In 2014, The United States Parachute Association recorded twenty-four fatalities due to skydiving. By comparison, there were roughly three million car-accident deaths in the same year.) In addition, many alcoholics that we, the authors, have personally met would say that they can quit any time they want—they've just not wanted to. So, while the lines appear bright and clear, in the real world, there are times when it's not as clear.

PERCEIVING STRESS

A lot of psychological self-care is managing stress. Knowing what stress is, where it comes from, and what you can do about it won't eliminate it from your world, but it is possible to reduce the effects. Stress evolved as a physiological need to focus on a short-term threat and defer potential long-term activities. If you don't survive the moment, you won't need the future.

The problem is that, as humans, we've subsumed this system and now apply the same system that was designed for living with lions in Africa to paying our mortgage, getting our kids into the "right" school, and dozens of other situations for which it wasn't originally designed. Instead of stress presenting occasionally and then receding into the background,

> Many people run with their stress systems on high all the time—and are suffering the long-term health consequences because of it.

many people run with their stress systems on high all the time—and are suffering the long-term health consequences because of it. We find ourselves running from activity to activity and project to project with sometimes unrealistic agendas for ourselves. This constant merry-go-round of activities can become unmanageable, yet many find it is difficult to step off and catch their breath.

So, in short, when you deconstruct stress, you find that it was designed for short-term survival. When you see how we are now using it, you find that we've managed to take our ability to predict, couple it to stress, and sustain it for non-life-threatening situations.

Sure, it would be awful to lose your house. However, will this kill you or your family? For most of us, the honest answer would be no. We could find other accommodations, whether that's renting a house, moving in with parents, or accepting support from our friends or community. What we've allowed to trigger a threat of death isn't that. Similarly, will our children's lives be ruined because they don't get into the right school? It might be harder for them if they don't have the right pedigree, sure. Will it kill them? Not likely.

While this is a well-reasoned argument, it doesn't necessarily mean that you can accept it. You may know that it's not the end of the world, a threat to your life, or anything close to that; but knowing that doesn't mean that you don't feel stress. Stress is an emotional response, and rationalization doesn't necessarily solve the problem—immediately.

However, just because the rational review of the situation doesn't solve the problem immediately doesn't mean that you shouldn't continue to do it. Emotions move more slowly than rational arguments. From a physiological point of view, some of the emotions trigger chemical releases that take a long time to be processed by your body. The other barrier to getting control of stress might be that you've been taught to play the worst-case scenario game wrong.

REPLAYING WORST-CASE SCENARIO

A friend of ours is a professional comedian. In one of his routines, he describes how his mother played the worst-case scenario game after hearing that he and his girlfriend had just got a puppy. There's no way to do this routine justice in written form, but, suffice it to say, the "logical conclusions" that his mother leapt to were neither logical nor reasonable. From getting a puppy his mother leapt to the fact that he'd never be able to take care of a child. Unfortunately, this is the way most people have been taught to play the worst-case scenario game.

Returning to the losing your house example above, someone playing the worst-case scenario game might say that their extended family will say no, they won't help you with shelter. There won't be any places to rent. You'll have to live in your car, but it's too cold to live in your car, so you'll die of hypothermia. Game over.

The problem with the way that the game is being played is that it's not realistic, nor does it consider the multiple levels of community resources designed to protect people. If you change the end of the game to "and then an asteroid crashes into the Earth, killing everyone and setting off the next ice age," you can sometimes disrupt your thinking long enough to realize that the way that you're playing the game isn't fair to you.

If you're playing the worst-case scenario game over something like a mortgage or a child getting into the right school, and you're losing by dying, you're probably playing it wrong. If you don't die, it's literally and figuratively not fatal, and you can recover.

Sometimes self-care is stopping those bad thinking patterns and accepting yourself, knowing that you will fail sometimes and realizing that failure is not the end of the world.

CHAPTER SUMMARY

- Coping strategies can reduce stress and improve psychological well-being.
- Coping strategies can be adaptive or maladaptive. The same activity can transition from adaptive to maladaptive depending on the control the coping strategy has over you.
- Compartmentalization is a necessary temporary coping strategy in some situations. The longer you compartmentalize, the greater the risk for psychological harm.
- Addictions can occur when previously adaptive coping strategies take control of the individual in increasingly harmful ways until you become powerless against the addiction.
- Stress evolved as a physiological need to focus on a short-term threat, typically a life-threatening event.
- We have applied that same stress to daily activities and events. If we review our stressors, we can determine if they are truly life-altering threats to you and your family's survival.
- It is possible to disrupt your thinking and stress long enough to realize that the way you are looking at life is like a bad game of worst-case scenario.

DISCUSSION QUESTIONS

1. What coping strategies do you most frequently use to help reduce your stress?
2. What activities or circumstances cause you the most stress? What would happen if the worse-case scenario occurred in one of these activities? Would you survive?

CHAPTER 8

Demands

Up to this point, we've discussed the ways that we can build our personal agency. This is like increasing your income. The more you pour in, the more you should have. However, as most of us have discovered, even more income doesn't necessarily make us richer. It's the balance between the inflow and outflow that determines the level of our personal agency. In this chapter, we'll talk about how to regulate the demands that are being placed on us to a level where we won't deplete our personal agency.

MANAGING RESERVES

Before we explore the demands that are placed on us, both by ourselves and by others, it's important to consider the need for reserves. It's possible for someone to say that they want to pour out everything they have at every moment so that they can do the most good in the world. However, it doesn't work out this way.

All of us can give more than we have for a short time. You can come home and be completely exhausted, the demands of the day completely draining your personal agency, but should a friend call in the midst of a crisis, you depend on your reserve of personal agency to meet the need. Afterward, you find yourself in a state where your personal agency and your reserves are spent; recovery from this state takes far more effort and time than it would have taken to recover from your day before the crisis.

We can compare our personal agency to a bank account. We may have a checking account for daily use, a savings account for emergencies or special events, and a credit card available should we need it. We can spend to the limit of our checking account but not touch our savings or use our credit card. We can replenish the checking account with our next paycheck, and our reserves are protected in case of an emergency.

If we spend everything we have in the bank, including our savings, and continue spending until our credit card is at the limit, we no longer have anything available in the event of an emergency. This is like using your personal agency reserves until you have nothing left. When you spend all you have, then spend more to impact your savings and credit cards, it is much harder to repay the debt and rebuild your savings. At times, it can feel like you cannot get caught up and back to the place you need your financial status to be. Using our personal agency and our reserves, like overspending, makes it more difficult to replenish your personal agency, because now you must pay an excessive debt to fully replenish yourself.

As we discussed in the chapters on self-care, you must have some capacity to invest in yourself so that you can have more energy. If you run yourself into the ground, you won't have any energy to get back up and rebuild your capacity.

However, more than that, many systems have a discontinuity at their stopping. To start an object not in motion, you must push through inertia. To get a jet engine started, you must apply a large amount of energy to get air flowing properly. Therefore, pilots on commercial aircraft typically start a much smaller auxiliary power unit (APU)—which is itself a small jet engine—so they can get the power to start one of the main engines.

When it comes to managing your personal agency reserves, you don't want to get so depleted that you end up with a deep sense of burnout. When you near this point, it is difficult to get restarted. You want to give what you can but still maintain enough for yourself. You do that by setting boundaries.

BOUNDARIES

Compassionate people are sometimes put off by the idea of boundaries. If you're setting—and maintaining—a boundary, then you're not completely available to others. That's right, you're not completely available to others: you're *appropriately* available to others. This balance is sometimes difficult to accept

> The need to establish limits to what you're willing and able to do for others is important to maintaining your reserves.

or maintain. The term "boundaries" was popularized by Henry Cloud and John Townsend in their popular book *Boundaries: When to Say Yes, How to Say No* (Cloud and Townsend 1992). The need to establish limits to what you're willing and able to do for others is important to maintaining your reserves.

There are two kinds of boundaries. The first kind of boundary is a defining boundary. This type of boundary is about how you define yourself. It's things you won't do because to do so would change who you are. The other kind of boundary is a protective boundary. Protective boundaries are not permanent; instead, they only exist for the necessary amount of time to allow you to recuperate, recover, rejuvenate, or heal (Townsend 2011).

Both types of boundaries are necessary to be able to maintain your relationship with other people. But how do you manage the demands you place on yourself?

SELF-DEMANDS: THE SHOULDS, OUGHTS, AND MUSTS

Not all demands are external. Some (and, in some cases, most) of the demands that are placed on you aren't from other people—at least not living people. Instead, they are about who you believe you should be, what you ought to do, and what you just must do.

These shoulds, oughts, and musts come from your experiences growing up and are often echoes of voices of people who are long since gone. Your mom said you should (or must) always make your bed. You've just "got to" prepare a meal for that family from church. You're expected at the going-away party for the coworker—at least, you expect that you "have to" be there.

Many people find that the demands to be a good parent or partner aren't expectations of other people but are instead demands they place on themselves. Frequently, people have multiple roles that each have a set of demands that people place on themselves. These roles may include being a good spouse, a good parent, a good child, a good employee, a good sibling, or a good friend; and the list goes on and on. The demands of these roles may conflict directly with one other. Meeting the demands that people consider "required" to meet their own expectations can be exhausting at best.

Consider for the moment the way that you "keep house." In most cases, there's an expectation about how a house will be kept that was created through your experiences as a child. You know how the house has to look before company comes over, because you saw your mother or father scramble to clean and organize the house to some standard that your grandparents had before their guests arrived. Whether you wanted to or not, you may have internalized this sense of the right way to keep house.

We have no illusions that we'll convince you in a few words to get rid of all or even most of these self-demands. However, we want to help you become aware that while these demands are real to you, they're not necessary.

As difficult or impossible it seems to be, when you're ready, you can get rid of them, or at least quiet them to a manageable level.

TRADE IMBALANCE

In our relationships with other people, there's always a trade imbalance. They're giving more to you than you're giving to them, or vice-versa. It's okay, because the value that is created when you support others—and when they support you—allows the trade to be imbalanced in a positive direction for both parties. Let us explain.

When you receive support, you're receiving something that you probably can't do for yourself—or you certainly can't do as easily as the person doing it for you. Consider someone holding a door for you while you're carrying bags of groceries. Can you open the door? Probably. However, will it be as easy for you to open the door as it was for them to hold the door? Probably not. Holding the door did not "cost" the door holder more than it helped the person who had it held open for them while they were carrying groceries. The good of the exchange was greater than the cost to the doer; the person holding the door also got the benefit of knowing they were able to help someone else.

The heart of the positive trade imbalance means that your support of others and their support of you should always end up better for both parties. There are, of course, some folks who don't reciprocate, but those typically aren't relationships you'll sustain.

> The heart of the positive trade imbalance means that your support of others and their support of you should always end up better for both parties.

The trade imbalance means you need to expect that you'll have some demands for supporting other people, but, simultaneously, those demands should be less than the support that you'll get from them. So, while some of the demands reciprocate the same kinds of support that you saw a few chapters ago, they shouldn't be as large as the benefits that you have received—and continue to receive.

PHYSICAL DEMANDS

Not all demands are emotional or psychological demands. Your body will demand a certain amount of sleep—which both rejuvenates and depletes the time available for personal agency. By chance, or by your body retaliating against you from a lack of sleep or high stress, you may find yourself ill. Until you're able to recover from the illness, your capacity will be necessarily reduced, and the demands for rest will be greater.

It's important to note that you may have a chronic illness or disease that won't go away, and instead it will need to be managed. In these cases, it's necessary for you to expend some of your personal agency managing the disease. This might be through doctors' appointments, medicines with negative side-effects, or the need to do physical exercise on a consistent basis. Whatever the need, chronic illnesses necessarily make demands upon you and can deplete your personal agency. It is important to recognize these demands and limit other demands to help preserve your reserve of personal agency.

PSYCHOLOGICAL DEMANDS

While physical demands lead to psychological demands, sometimes the demands are directly psychological. These demands fall roughly into two categories: rational and emotional. Note that these are not rational and irrational. Emotional demands aren't inherently irrational. In fact, our subconscious thoughts and feelings are more often insightful than any rational thought we might be able to put into a topic.

Rational

Rational demands are the "mental" work, the thoughts and processing, that are completed each day. These rational demands can lead to physical demands, or they may be separate processes that are encountered, problems solved, or ideas developed.

Rob has worked as a software developer and still develops software from time to time today. Depending on what he's working on and how many interruptions he gets, he can spend most of his day in the psychological state of flow. Though it is immensely productive, it can also be incredibly draining (Kotler 2014). The demands for remaining in flow are high and so are the rewards. The research supports that, in the long term—after a recovery period—flow will increase his personal agency, both in the specific skill of development and emotionally.

Roy Baumeister and his colleagues have shown through their research that your capacity is temporarily impaired after doing cognitively taxing tasks (Baumeister and Tierney 2011). The brain has a fixed capacity for consuming energy, and it can only do so much. When it's preoccupied—or was recently preoccupied—with solving problems, organizing information, or doing other executive functions, it has less capacity to process and filter information.

Mental processing demands—even relatively straightforward and logical demands—temporarily reduce your remaining personal agency.

Emotional

Emotional demands take a variety of forms, including the day-to-day energy spent on personal relationships and understanding one another. Other times, emotional demands result from difficult or unexpected situations that can rapidly deplete our personal agency.

Anyone who has been through an emotionally troubling time can tell you the massive weight that they feel. It feels as if the hole in the bottom of the personal agency tub is larger than the tub itself. Even when surrounded by people who are supporting you, you still feel like it's not enough.

DECISION MAKING CRITERIA

How does one decide which demands to meet and which to allow to pass by? Where do we draw the boundaries that allow us to be the person we want to be and still maintain our personal agency at a healthy level?

One aspect to consider is whether the recipient of our efforts receives more than the activity's demands cost us to give. Consider making homemade yeast cinnamon rolls for breakfast Christmas morning. The demand of making the rolls Christmas Eve before going to bed may be an activity the family does together and a tradition that everyone treasures and enjoys. The benefits are greater than the demand costs. On the other hand, if someone stays up late making cinnamon rolls because it is an expectation, either internal or external, they are exhausted in the morning. No one really notices whether the rolls are homemade or Poppin' Fresh, and the cost of the demand ends up being greater than the positive effect for the recipients. The same demand, making cinnamon rolls, has a different impact on the giver. In the first case, the benefit is greater than the cost. In the second scenario, the cost is greater.

Ultimately, the criterion for whether you should honor a demand or gently say no is based on a simple value equation. Will it cost you more of your personal agency than it will return? The return can be to you or to others, but fundamentally, will this add value to your world or take it away? If it's going to take away value overall, then you should pass. Learning to ascertain whether something will add value or subtract it is sometimes hard.

PERSPECTIVES

Demands may be external or internal; they may be someone else's expectations or our own. The demands on our personal agency can be significantly impacted by our perspective. Do we look at our demands as something we must do or something we get to do?

Terri finds that the demands of being a parent can have very different impacts depending on her perspective. After a long day, the surprise of needing to go out and get supplies for a last-minute project may deplete her personal agency; yet on other days, it may be a great adventure to create something with one of the children. The difference is her perspective. On the days she feels like she must do something to live up to her expectations of being a good mom, the task feels exhausting. On the days she considers it a gift to get to provide help to and work with her child to complete a project, the task feels life-giving. The activity itself does not change; her perspective changes the impact to her personal agency.

It is the impact of perspective that allows people to truly have joy and increase their personal agency in the face of a demand rather than experience the demand as a drain on their personal agency.

CHAPTER SUMMARY

- We can regulate the demands placed on us to keep from depleting our personal agency.

- We can give more than we have if we need to, but we have to realize that replenishing our personal agency from this state takes extra time and support.
- We manage our demands by setting boundaries that help us be appropriately available to others.
- Self-demands are frequently based on our past. We can evaluate them to determine if the shoulds, oughts, and musts are actually necessary.
- Demands may be physical or psychological, both of which must be evaluated to determine what you are able to complete.
- Determining the cost to complete an activity should be weighed against the value it brings to others and ourselves, and it is an important step in deciding what we should do.
- The perspective of *getting* to do something is often the polar opposite of feeling like you *have* to do it.

DISCUSSION QUESTIONS

1. How might you manage your demands in ways that support having a personal agency reserve to draw upon in a crisis?
2. Boundaries keep us from being completely available to others and move us to being appropriately available to others. What criteria can you use to maintain a boundary that supports you being appropriately available?
3. When did the demands you placed on yourself result in a trade imbalance, where the negative impact was more than the benefit? How could you have recognized the trade imbalance earlier?
4. Perspective can change a demand from something we have to do into something we get to do. What is something that you feel like you *have* to do that you might consider something you *get* to do if your personal agency reserves were not running low?

CHAPTER 9

Capacity for Personal Agency

Except for a short discussion explaining how burnout works, we've carefully avoided returning to a discussion about the perception of personal agency. Instead, we've focused on our simple model of personal agency and the idea that burnout happens when your personal agency is empty. In this chapter, we refine this definition to explain how a lack of perceived personal agency might appear—and the implications that has for trying to prevent and recover from burnout. In the following chapters, we dig into more details about how our perception can be distorted or inaccurate and what we can do to make it more accurate.

BURNOUT WITHOUT DEPLETION

When you model burnout as the depletion of personal agency, you can't have a situation where you believe that you are effective and still have burnout. The model doesn't work when you encounter burnout despite massive incoming results, support, and self-care. There is, however, a small gap in the preceding model and burnout, and that is perception.

> Burnout doesn't operate in the world of reality. It operates in the world of perception.

In the model of personal agency, we dealt with reality, and burnout doesn't operate in the world of reality. It operates in the world of perception. As a result, your personal agency might be high—as it is for many high-performers—and, at the same time, you may perceive your personal agency as very low.

We've discussed many of the components of perception, but we've not squarely addressed the traps of feedback and comparison that can land you into a gap between reality and perception.

Feedback

Peak performers are grown through feedback. It's not ten thousand hours of practice that create the master. It's ten thousand hours of purposeful practice (Ericsson and Pool 2016). The difference between just participating in practice and being purposeful is the desire to find feedback, either intrinsically or through a coach, that leads to better performance and different approaches. There are four ways that feedback can go wrong. The first way is to not have any feedback. The second is to have random feedback. Third, bad feedback sometimes happens that can leave you with the wrong impression. Finally, you can discount good feedback, and miss the feedback you need.

Lack of Feedback

The most effective way to create burnout is to have someone passionately engaged in solving an important problem and then not give them any feedback about whether they're being successful. Whether it's the writer who struggles in obscurity or the comedian who works night after night on stages for little more than the cost of a hotel and the gas that will take them to their next club, the lack of feedback creates the opportunity to believe that nothing is changing.

> The lack of feedback creates the opportunity to believe that nothing is changing.

Sure, the writer gets reviews or has a few conversations with people who laud over their work, but where are the sales? The comedian gets a laugh, but are they laughing more or are they laughing less, and why haven't they been able to get the booking at the next larger facility—which will lead to more pay?

When you rob someone of feedback, you don't allow them to see that they're making progress, and therefore they may believe that they have no personal agency—that they're not making a difference.

Random Feedback

More maddening than no feedback—but less effective at creating burnout—is getting random feedback. Some attendees of your session give you top marks, and others give you raspberries. You have sales in some markets and not others. Comedians bring down the house in Seattle, but the next week in Toledo is like a scene from a morgue.

Inconsistency of feedback makes it hard for us to draw a trend line. Consider the debate about global warming. Because every day has a variation of temperature, how can you intuitively tell whether things are getting warmer or not? The fact that there is a large degree of randomness in the feedback means that our human brains can't see the subtle patterns that are emerging. Without a clear trend line heading up, we may be headed for burnout.

Bad Feedback

Sometimes the right thing isn't perceived that way. Sometimes folks like Oprah Winfrey are fired from their TV station job because they didn't fit the existing mold. The feedback may be clear and consistent, but what if it's wrong? What if the feedback is telling you that you're not making a difference, that it will never work, or that you're not good enough? Eventually, the perceived personal agency you have will crumble under the weight of such negative feedback.

It doesn't matter whether the feedback is correct or incorrect. It does matter that you can't do anything about it and stay true to your beliefs, either because there's nothing actionable in the feedback or because you feel with all your heart you are moving in the wrong direction. Enough bad feedback and you may lose your focus on the end goals and start to look at the people near you.

Discounting Good Feedback

When our internal perspective doesn't match the perspective of others, our natural tendency is to trust our own perceptions. Sometimes this is good because the feedback we're getting really is bad feedback. However, other times the feedback is good, and our perception is wrong. One of the ways that this frequently surfaces for those struggling with burnout is that someone says that we're doing a good job—and what we feel is that we're not.

Because of the disconnect, we discount the feedback that says we are doing good, that we are getting results, that we are making a difference because it doesn't match our previous perception of the situation or expectations of ourselves. The result is that we can underestimate the results we're seeing and, in the process, short change our effectiveness.

Comparison

You may be doing great work. You may be just killing it in your world. However, when you compare yourself to others, you may find that you feel like you're losing ground. Unfortunately, the objective measurements aren't the ones that matter. The ones that matter are how you feel—and that's a comparison game. If you have car in a world where few do, you consider yourself rich. In a place where everyone has two new cars, you'll feel behind—even if, by world standards, you're very affluent (Kahneman 2011).

In our world today, we have social networks that allow us to stay connected with colleagues and friends. These are a great benefit to society, but they come at a cost. Just as it's easy to believe that rates of violence have increased, because awareness of vio-

> Our life is the only life for which we get to see both the good and the bad.

lent events has increased, so, too, do we believe that other people's lives are better than our own. The actual violent crime rate is down from a high in the 1990s (FBI 2018), but most people would say that there is more crime today than in the past. Our life is the only life for which we get to see both the good and the bad. Everyone else's lives, as captured via social media, is like a highlight reel. It only has the good parts and often hides, ignores, or excludes the bad parts.

Facebook

Robin Dunbar's work indicates that humans are capable of about 150 stable social relationships (Dunbar 1993). Most people today have more than 150 Facebook friends. The natural conclusion is that these aren't stable social relationships. That is, these are not the tribe members with whom we would have had continuous personal interaction. Instead, it may be the 1,000 people that we are acquainted with, now or at some time in our life, whose lives we get to peer into.

We get to watch graduations. We get glimpses of their vacations. We're virtually there for the vino. However, with few exceptions, we're not there when they fail or when they flounder. We skip past the months looking for the job to see their new, coveted role. We miss the incident that taught their teenager about danger or drugs. We're not allowed to know about the problems with alcohol.

The problem is that when we compare our personal progress against the progress of the people we see on Facebook or Instagram, our life doesn't look so good. We are faced with the reality that our hair isn't always that good, and our life doesn't feel that amazing.

LinkedIn

The professional equivalent to Facebook is LinkedIn. We get to see work anniversaries. We get to see how folks are getting promotions. They're published. They got a new patent. Their organization was just named to some prestigious position on a list that you've not heard of.

In your world, you know that you can't seem to figure out what you need to do to get to the next rung of the corporate ladder. You're struggling to keep your small business afloat, wondering if next month you'll have to look for a "real" job.

Some days you start to wonder, "Am I done? Is this all I'm going to do?" It seems that other people have good things happening to them every day, but they never seem to happen to you. This is an unfair comparison. In the end analysis, you're probably seeing the same struggles as others—but the successes of so many connections show up in your email inbox every week, and your world seems to be standing still.

WHAT ARE YOU MEASURING?

Without delving into the idea of what your personal goals are, why you do what you do, it's important to consider your expectations of yourself and what you're measuring. Sometimes we're measuring velocity—that is, how much we're moving the needle; however, this is necessarily going to be small at first. The second-order effect of how much we're changing our acceleration is perhaps a more important early measure.

Velocity

If you want to know how fast you're going to get to Cleveland, you really need to know your velocity and the distance. If you know what your goal is, and you know how fast you're going, you can track how long it will take to get there. Unfortunately, for most of us, there are two issues. First, unlike places on a map, measuring the distance between where we are and where we want to go isn't a known fixed quantity. We can guess as to what the distance to our goal is—but we can't know the exact distance.

Velocity is based on our ability to read the feedback, and, as we discussed above, feedback is difficult to get right. Consider a growing puppy. You see the puppy every day—and little change is noticed. However, if you take regular weekly photos, you begin to get an idea of the changes that are happening. Take the pictures over months and you get a better idea.

Our minds are not, unfortunately, pictures. Our memories tend to get distorted and rewritten as we recall them. More than that, we want to know our progress now. We want to know if we're moving toward the goal quickly. However, the only way to get a good sense is to wait a long time so the difference becomes more obvious—or to make it clearer what you're measuring against.

Taking the picture of the puppy next to a fixed sized object—in relatively the same pose—makes even small differences easier to see. The fixed reference point gives us a way to measure our velocity, even if we still need to allow adequate time.

In our professional and personal goals, we rarely keep the endpoint fixed or give ourselves the regular check-ins that allow us to see how we're making progress. That's why ideas like "working out loud" are such powerful allies in our fight to avoid burnout (Stepper 2015). When we work out loud, we create the opportunity for others to share their perspectives with us and help us know when we are making progress and when we need to adjust our course.

Acceleration

The challenge with making changes over a long period of time is that to do so we necessarily hide the rate of change in velocity itself. We may have seen the puppy grow only a few pounds and barely an inch in the first few weeks, but in the second month the puppy adds ten pounds a week. So, we can't just look at the velocity as a constant. We must evaluate it from the perspective of how fast it is changing. Though puppies rarely shrink, we can certainly feel like friction is beginning to slow our velocity to our goal.

Sometimes it's not our perception of velocity toward the goal that leads us to burnout. Sometimes it's the belief that our velocity is slowing—and moving toward zero. It's not that we're not seeing progress, it's that we don't believe we'll continue to see progress. Here, too, regular markers can help us see that we are indeed making progress. Though our velocity may be slowing, it's still more than fast enough to get us over our own personal goal line—wherever we define it to be.

CHAPTER SUMMARY

- Burnout is directly impacted by our perception of our personal agency more than our actual personal agency.
- Feedback is important in the perception of personal agency. To be effective, feedback needs to be consistent and valid.
- No feedback, inconsistent feedback, and bad feedback can lead to false feelings of inefficacy or failure.
- It is difficult to find objective measures when we compare ourselves to others. The view we have of our own world is very different from the highlight reel we see of other people's lives on social media or in conversation.
- The rate (velocity) at which we are moving toward our goals is difficult to measure. Ideas like "working out loud" can create opportunities for others to provide feedback and help us see our progress.
- Making progress toward our goals is important, and acknowledging this progress is necessary even when we find our velocity slowing.

DISCUSSION QUESTIONS

1. How does your perception of your personal agency align with the feedback you receive?
2. Think about feedback you have received in an area that you struggle with. How is this feedback consistent and correct or inconsistent and wrong?
3. You only see other people's highlight reel on social media or hear about the amazing things their families are doing. What does your highlight reel look like? How is this different than how you perceive your life on a daily basis?

Personal Value

Intertwined with our accomplishments is our personal value. We believe that we're valuable when we're achieving things. We believe that we have value when we're doing good work. We may even believe we are valuable based on someone else's opinion of us. However, the more we disentangle our inherent worth from what we do, the less susceptible we will become to burnout—and the more we can do to recover.

As a human race, we've been so shaped by scarcity that we feel its pull, even today. We believe that we're safer if we're better. We believe that, to be safe, we must be the best. We must be the best in everything, because we don't know what we must be the best in. As a result, we live in the shadow of scarcity, and that makes us susceptible to burnout.

SCARCITY

The struggle for survival has been with us since long before Charles Darwin and "survival of the fittest" (Darwin 1859). While we enjoy the fruits of our ancestors' mastery of agriculture and are, by all material measures, living in a time of great abundance, the seed of scarcity still lives within each of us.

We see scarcity raise its head when we compete with others and lose. We wonder if we're enough. We wonder what's wrong with us and why we couldn't win. Scarcity confronts us when we see the sweeping transformations that technology and innovation bring—and we don't know how it will turn out. Uber and Lyft have radically disrupted the transportation business, and taxi drivers everywhere wonder how they'll continue to survive. Self-driving cars have automotive dealers worrying whether individuals will still own cars. Gas station owners watch the transformation to electric cars and are worried how they'll survive if cars start running on electricity rather than gasoline.

Fear is the root of scarcity. It's a fear that we'll not be able to provide the essentials for ourselves and our families. Of course, the essentials aren't always the same. Essentials should be food and shelter. But in today's Western economies, other things like a mobile phone are near necessities if you hope to climb above the day-to-day struggle and find your way to a semblance of security.

By recognizing scarcity for what it is, our fear of not having enough, we can realize that we've transformed this into a fear of not *being* enough. The opposite of scarcity isn't abundance. The opposite of scarcity isn't our coffers overflowing. The opposite of scarcity is simply being enough.

> The opposite of scarcity isn't abundance. The opposite of scarcity is simply being enough.

ENOUGH

In some situations, you won't be enough to be the very best. You may not be the world's best piano player, violinist, nuclear scientist, and so on. However, that doesn't mean you aren't enough to survive. Somewhere, our fears have become twisted and confused. We've learned that if we don't win—at everything—then we're not good enough.

When we, the authors, apply to a conference to speak and aren't accepted, it can be a blow. We think, why aren't we enough? Why is it that we can't get a speaking slot when so many other people are able to? Walking down the path a bit, we start to think perhaps everyone will forget who we are and what we do, and people reaching out to engage us for consulting or products will stop calling, and we won't have any more work. At this point, we've worried well beyond just this rejection; we've tried to project that rejection into the future to predict what will happen and what path we may be on.

We forget that the same day (and sometimes even the same hour) that the rejection came we received other positive news. We were given an award or selected for some honor. We focused too narrowly on the one area where we didn't win.

In today's world, there are a multitude of categories in which we can find ourselves falling short of being enough to win—or at least to coming close to winning. We may feel physically fit until the Ironman crosses our path. We may be comfortable with our intelligence until we meet a rocket scientist. We may be a great keynote presenter and still feel like we're not enough for some conference that didn't select us.

The categories are endless, and we'll always be able to find a category—or, in truth, numerous categories—where we're not the best. If we were the best at every category, we wouldn't be human. So, when we compare ourselves in categories and find that we fall short, this should be expected, even if it's not pleasant (Keller and Papasan 2013; Meier 2010).

The problem is that we're using the wrong measuring stick. We're looking at whether we win or are among the best instead of asking the different question: whether we're enough or not. Is it OK that we don't convert every prospect into a customer? Is it OK that we don't win every race? The answer should be yes, though sometimes we focus too narrowly. We decide that if we aren't perfect, if we don't win all the time, then we're not enough.

However, this is a misunderstanding. Inside of each of us is the capacity that we need to be enough—enough to live, survive, and even thrive. If we continue to fall prey to fear, we'll believe that someone will be prettier, faster, smarter, richer, and so on, and that we'll never be enough to survive and be happy. There will always be someone who can be perceived as "more" or "better." Learning that being enough is, well, *enough* is a step beyond the fear of scarcity.

HUMAN BEING

We're called human beings. However, for too many people, we don't believe we have an identity if we're not doing things. As we ascribe our value to what we're doing, we miss that we're inherently valuable even when we're not doing anything.

> As we ascribe our value to what we're doing, we miss that we're inherently valuable even when we're not doing anything.

The world applies labels to people based on what they've gotten done and what their profession is. They're a repairman, a firefighter, a police officer, or an entrepreneur. But behind each of these labels is a man or woman. We're whole, complete, and important people, even when we're not doing anything.

When you speak with folks who are in the final quarter of their lives or on their death beds, you hear about how they missed out on relationships and connections—rarely do you hear about the business deal that was missed.

SELF-ESTEEM

There are those that think too highly of themselves—they're called narcissists. They are highly susceptible to burnout because they believe that they can change anything. They believe that they have limitless power and that circumstances and chance don't play into their success. This creates great stress when they do fail because they believe that it can't be their fault.

They're susceptible to burnout because when they fail, and chance does raise its head, they must cope with the change in their worldviews. They've got to accept that their self-image of having limitless power isn't accurate— or believe that the failure is caused by someone else. If someone else is to blame, then it wasn't that they weren't sufficiently powerful but rather that they were thwarted. The collapse of their belief in their limitless power threatens their belief in their personal effectiveness.

On the other side of the same spectrum are those who think so little of themselves that they're called insecure. They're the people who are always second-guessing if they're good enough or if they'll be able to do anything. They start from a position of near or complete helplessness. They're already in burnout or have learned helplessness or some other similar afflic-tion. These people are already trapped in a low orbit around burnout. They're already circling the feeling of never being able to make their goals.

Dr. Spock in *The Common Sense Book of Baby and Child Care* implores us to speak to our children and support them being individualists—and the reports are that he later regretted this advice (Spock 1946; Csikszentmihalyi 1997). Parents were able to raise independent children, but they couldn't stand to be around the children they raised. They had so coddled and elevat-ed their children's self-esteem that their children felt themselves to be better than their parents.

The safe place with self-esteem isn't on either end of the spectrum but rather in the middle line, where you recognize that you can get things done but you're not all-powerful. When you're able to see yourself as both powerful and vulnerable, you can become more comfortable with who you are.

> When you're able to see yourself as both powerful and vulnerable, you can become more comfortable with who you are.

BEING COMFORTABLE IN YOUR OWN SKIN

Becoming comfortable in your own skin comes from an understanding and appreciation of who you are. Consider toddlers and preschoolers: they rarely worry about what they are supposed to look like or believe. They believe they are a princess or an adventurer, and their personal beliefs are all that matter to them. They are comfortable with who they believe themselves to be. As we grow up, we begin to worry about what other people think and what they expect from us. This concern changes our comfort level with who we are and even who we want to be.

One of the first steps in being comfortable in your own skin is recognizing the person you want to be. Recognizing that you are neither the best nor the worst and accepting that idea is not always easy. Society can lead us to believe that we are lacking in some area; we find ourselves in a constant state of needing to be more or better just to be enough. When you accept that you are valuable and appreciate the good and the bad—that everyone has both good and bad—you become more comfortable in your own skin. Being comfortable in your own skin allows you to be yourself; you continue to work toward your goals, grow, and learn. In the process, you appreciate who you are and your value in the world today.

CHAPTER SUMMARY

- The opposite of scarcity is not abundance; it is having enough. This is frequently translated into being enough.
- Being enough as a human being does not mean being the best or succeeding at everything we do.
- Accepting that we are both powerful and vulnerable, both good and bad, allows us to become more comfortable with who we really are.
- Realizing that we are enough is a key step in seeing the value we bring to the world.

DISCUSSION QUESTIONS

1. In what areas do you see yourself as an expert? Is it possible that there are people more skilled in these areas? Does that lessen your value?
2. Believing that we are enough can be difficult; the truth is we are all enough. What are some areas that you know you are enough?
3. Consider the person you want to be. (This is different from the things you want to accomplish.) What are the key characteristics you see in yourself that help you achieve the goal of being who you want to be?

CHAPTER 11

Need for Connection

There's a reason why solitary confinement is the worst thing we can do to prisoners. There's a reason why the frail, hairless apes have conquered the planet. The reason has to do with our ability to connect. Our connections with other humans are quite literally how we managed to rise above the other species. We tamed the Earth and shot for the stars because we've learned how to create shared understanding. We can do so much because we do it together. It all starts with our ability to predict what others have in mind.

> We tamed the Earth and shot for the stars because we've learned how to create shared understanding.

MIND READING

It's not hard to understand what a trick mind reading is. The ability to seemingly peer into the thoughts of another human is nothing short of supernatural. After all, mind reading and telepathy are the stuff of science fiction, even today. Humans all have a bit of this science fiction in us. We can read others' minds, at least a little.

In our imaginations, we can see what we believe to be a perfect replica of what is in another person's mind—where there's no question or ambiguity about what someone else is thinking and feeling. Sometimes, we later discover that we couldn't have been more wrong. We become painfully aware of the limitations of our mind-reading capabilities. Though we're frequently right about what others are thinking, we're not always right. Though we can often complete someone else's thoughts, there are painful lapses where we make mistakes and our ability to read someone else's mind falters.

Because of the gap between our mind-reading ability and perfection, we discount the truly amazing superpower that it is. We lose the marvel that the process can even occur at all. However, this is a trait that seems unique to the human condition.

Dogs can read humans' minds, but they cannot do the same for other dogs. That is, dogs can't read other dogs' minds except in narrow circumstances, like a call for play (Brown and Vaughan 2009). While birds and fish are able to operate in flocks and schools without any outside coordinating force, no one would argue that a fish knows what every other fish in the school is thinking.

Our ability to create shared intention—to create one shared thought across multiple people—is accomplished through mind reading. Jonathan Haidt believes this led to the creation of our language (Haidt 2012). While much has been done to dissect our ability to read minds, we still don't know for sure how it functions (Nichols and Stitch 2003). We know only that it seems unique to our human condition and that it has allowed us to collectively build on one another's work.

THE FLOW OF TRUST

From our capacity to mind read, we find the path that leads us to our innate need for connection. As we realize that we evolved to have a unique and special gift in mind reading, we are endowed with a skill that leads from trust through to intimacy—or deep connection—with other humans.

Trust

Our ability to read the minds of others allows us to develop a level of trust that our predictions about what they think are valid, and that others in our group will behave in a way that matches our expectations. This trust is learned: we learn we can trust that our predictions of their behavior are valid.

The problem is that our predictions aren't always right. We will be betrayed. However, over time, the impact of betrayal is outweighed by the benefits conferred on us by trusting. Trusting that we know how others will behave provides us advantages that reduce the friction of transactions and make us more productive (Fukuyama 1995).

In short, we believe that we're safe because we believe we know—relatively speaking—what's going to happen.

Safety

Historically, trusting in our predictions of others allowed us to let down our guard and believe that those we trust will protect us while we sleep so that we'll do the same thing for them in turn. We believe that they'll protect our children, because we'll protect theirs. This reduces our individual burden and creates an environment of safety.

Thus, our increasing trust increases our feelings of safety. It is this perception of safety that allows us to enter greater degrees of vulnerability.

Vulnerability

Vulnerability at first seems like a bad thing. It feels like we should all be completely invulnerable. However, this is an illusion and a dangerous one at that. Invulnerability presumes that we don't need anyone. While vulnerability invites us to connect with others for mutual benefit—and some degree of risk—invulnerability invites us to go at it alone (Townsend 2011).

> It's through our vulnerabilities that we learn to be intimate.

Humans are not the strongest animals. Nor do we have the sharpest teeth or the warmest, most insulating fur. We are, in nearly every way, more vulnerable than most of our animal kingdom littermates. It's through our vulnerabilities that we learn to be intimate.

Intimacy

When you're so connected with someone that you feel no need for barriers between you, you've found intimacy. We're not speaking of not knowing the boundaries and edges of your existence and another person's existence as a separate person. It's not like two people are fused or there is confusion about who is who. We're speaking of a state where you feel no need to defend yourself from the other person. Without the need for defenses or pretenses, you can truly be yourself.

Nor are we speaking only of intimacy in the physical—sexual—sense. We're speaking instead of a state where you feel no need to protect yourself from another. Intimacy can be physical, emotional, or intellectual.

Intimate people, with their guard nearly completely dropped among themselves, don't invest energy in defending themselves against the people that they're intimate with. As a result, they have more energy to do things in the world or protect themselves from outside forces. The benefits of feeling like you belong and saving energy by not needing to defend yourself are so great that one could easily wonder why intimacy is so hard to achieve. The answer is that the path through vulnerability and giving up the illusion of invulnerability is so difficult.

PUTTING THE WORLD BACK TOGETHER

For all the good science has done, there is at least one bad thing. Science has separated us from the animal kingdom, from our world, and, to some extent, from ourselves. Science has taught us that atoms and molecules are separate from other atoms and molecules. Yet, at the same time, we recognize that the atoms form bonds (literally) to other atoms to connect into chains called molecules. We recognize that molecules fit together and connect with other molecules.

At an atomic level, the universe itself is wired for connection. We divided things into the parts, and along the way, we lost something. An atom by itself is rather boring. Even a molecule by itself is boring. What happens, however, when you put together millions and billions of atoms and molecules? In the right ratios, life is created. You create limitless possibilities that we can't even imagine. All the way down to the smallest creature, the universe itself is alive because of the connections that are made.

PHILOSOPHY AND RELIGION

What does philosophy and religion have to say about our need for connection? Zen master Yasutani Roshi expresses it this way: "The fundamental delusion of humanity is to suppose that I am here, and you are out there" (Cacioppo and Patrick 2008). Martin Buber expresses the fundamental tension that we're separate as "I and Thou," which is the title of his book on the need to view things—particularly people—in relationships instead of as disconnected objects (Buber and Smith 1937).

Zen master Mr. Zan expresses the need for connection differently. He says, "There's only one issue in the world. It's the reintegration of matter and mind" (Scharmer 2009). Here, the fundamental split is our belief that our mind and the way we think is one thing, and the way that the universe functions is something completely different. We believe that our bodies are separate from our brains, that they're simply brain transportation devices. The more we learn about neuroscience, the more we learn that the brain and the body aren't as separate as we once believed (Kotler and Wheal 2017). From that, we can learn to be more compassionate to ourselves— and to others.

COMPASSION AND ALTRUISM

Compassion is a word that is thrown around but one for which most people don't have a clear, firm definition. Empathy and altruism are often treated as synonyms, when, in truth, they are not the same thing.

Empathy is a simple acknowledgment of shared understanding. To say that you have empathy for someone is saying that you understand—on some level—what they're going through. Though, typically, empathy is used with negative feelings, empathy itself is about understanding the experience of another—whether it's a positive or negative state. This differs from the linguistically similar sympathy. With empathy, you're forming a connection, moving closer, and putting yourself in the same space—even if only metaphorically. With sympathy, you're basically saying, "Sucks to be you." You believe you understand the other person, but at the same time, you're quite glad that it's them and not you.

Compassion is seeing the suffering of someone and desiring to alleviate or minimize that suffering. Compassion moves further than empathy for others by attempting to reduce or eliminate their pain. Compassion requires empathy but doesn't stop there. It doesn't require a specific action. It only requires the desire to reduce the suffering. You can express this desire in a multitude of ways.

Altruism is further down this continuum, where your desire to relieve someone's suffering is so strong that you're willing to accept possible consequences yourself. Altruism is an important part in our social evolution and part of the reason why we've become the dominant life form on the planet, yet it's also rare (Pinker 2002).

From an evolutionary standpoint, altruism makes sense when the genes that led to altruism are likely to exist in those that you're sacrificing yourself for. Your family members are likely to carry the same gene, so a single sacrifice that saves multiple others is a net win in evolutionary genetics. Obviously, fatal consequences of altruism are an extreme example, though this was the case in the dawn of our civilization. Altruism used to mean dying for someone else. Today, it has taken on a broader meaning of any sacrifice, not necessarily the ultimate sacrifice. As altruism exists today, there is still a lethal risk at times, as police officers and firefighters put themselves in harm's way to protect us.

Embedded into altruism is the connectedness that we all face in our survival as a species. Compassion is the stepping stone to altruism. Compassion and altruism are also the path that creates the greatest risk for burnout. If you're literally risking your life, you want to know that you're making a difference. After all, you only get one life, and you want to know that if you're putting it at risk, it's for something that matters.

> Compassion and altruism are also the path that creates the greatest risk for burnout. If you're literally risking your life, you want to know that you're making a difference.

DIALOGUE

The path to connection runs through dialogue. While we can use our mind-reading superpowers to infer someone's intent and get a general sense for what they're thinking relatively reliably without language, language allows us to refine this understanding. The use of language starts at conversation—the ability to convey basic information. However, to truly share intention, you move to a deeper form of communication that includes intent, belief, and values.

Conversation is the process by which we can share information. There are classes and programs on how to communicate effectively that focus on a myriad of different skills and techniques to reduce the number of errors created in the gap between the speaker and the listener. These techniques go by different names, including the popular active listening technique (Gordon 1970). However, fundamentally, the techniques you learn about communicating more effectively are about correcting the inevitable errors in the exchange of information. While this is a necessary component of the process of connecting with someone else, it's insufficient on its own.

Sometimes, people will say that they initiated a dialogue on a given topic. This should—but may not—be a higher level of communication that goes beyond a transactional understanding and instead speaks to the very principles and values that each person in the conversation holds dear. Dialogue is characterized by an ability to get past the surface and work through the issues that lie underneath (Isaacs 1999).

Most of the time when communicating, we aren't conscious about the interaction patterns that are happening. Most of the time, we're following the patterns that we've become accustomed to rather than being fully conscious and aware of the moment. We settle into familiar patterns and automatic defensive routines. Someone says something that is threatening to us—or, rather, that we interpret as threatening to us—and we react defensively without thinking.

These defensive routines get in the way of real connection and prevent us from truly understanding the other person's meaning. Our goal is to have a safe, open, and vulnerable conversation that allows us to experience as much of the other person's perspectives as possible. This moves us together toward a single perceptive experience, which may include combining both perspectives rather than deciding one or the other is right. This requires conscious awareness of our dialogues and how we're feeling.

CONNECTION THROUGH DIALOGUE

Dialogue is how we connect with one another. Our humanity rests on our ability to connect with one another. Since humans discovered language, we've been trying to refine how we can enhance our mind-reading capabilities and more fully understand those around us. Dialogue is the quickest and easiest way for all of us humans to understand one another and, through this understanding, feel the connection that we so deeply need.

CHAPTER SUMMARY

- While we may be able to complete someone else's thoughts, we cannot know for certain what they are thinking or feeling. We cannot literally read someone's mind.
- We can create a shared intention; this shared intention builds on our innate need for connection.
- Through the development of trust and safety, we are able to become vulnerable with others.
- Vulnerability leads to intimacy, which is key to deep relationships.
- Compassion is a step beyond understanding: compassion is an understanding of another's situation combined with a desire to alleviate their suffering.

- We connect with one another through dialogue, learning to understand one another, and building trust, vulnerability, and true intimacy.

DISCUSSION QUESTIONS

1. Who are the people that you can communicate with without needing words?

2. List a few people who you have developed trust in and feel safe with. In what ways do you feel safe with them?

3. Consider the people you believe you have the most intimacy with, whether the intimacy is physical, emotional, or intellectual. How does that intimacy make dialogue easier and more meaningful?

CHAPTER 12

Integrated Self-Image

his chapter is a difficult one to write and an even more difficult one to read. It's countercultural. It doesn't make sense. However, we ask that you hang with us because the rewards of getting this one thing right go well beyond preventing burnout. Understanding how to develop a single self-image—an integrated one—is an immense source of internal strength and resilience.

SEPARATE

We've been taught by our culture that we're not one person but rather several people. We've been taught that we're one person at church. We're a different person with our friends on a Saturday night. We're yet another person with our families. Don't forget that person we take to work. We've been taught that we're one person when we're good and a different person when we're bad—which is intriguing when you can be both good and bad to different people at the same time. We've become fascinated with how we can compartmentalize, dissect, and separate ourselves from ourselves.

Somehow, we've sold ourselves on this idea that it's possible that we can be one person in one place at one time with one group—and be a completely different person with a different group at a different place and a different time. However, this is just a surface illusion, like a mirage of water on a hot street.

Lewin's Legacy

The illusion that we're different people in different contexts is a misinterpretation of Kurt Lewin's work. Lewin is a famous psychologist that said behavior is a function of both person and environment (Lewin 1936). That is, behavior is influenced by both the person's essence—who they are—and the environment that you put them in.

Said differently, given the right conditions, you can get anyone to do almost anything. Conversely, some people will be able to resist even terrifying circumstances and retain their behavior. The key is that Lewin's function is an opaque function. You don't know with certainty which circumstances or environments will drive behavior, nor do you know that you won't do bad behaviors.

Imagine yourself in a very bad spot for a moment. You've lost your job, and you've been separated from the support of your extended family. You've exhausted your financial resources, and you're hungry. However, so is your young child. You're presented an opportunity to steal—without getting caught—some bread and milk. Would you do it?

People most often initially react with an immediate no. That's not the kind of person that they are. It's not something that they would do. As they let the situation settle in, they begin to wonder. If we leave the situation with people long enough, most will eventually admit that, in those circumstances and for those reasons, they would steal.

At the same time, they won't label themselves a "thief"—nor should they. Their circumstances created the conditions right for a specific behavior. Does it mean that they are a different person when they are in that situation? In one sense, yes, which we'll address in a moment, but in another sense, no. They're still the same flesh and blood that we believe would "never" steal.

The fundamental misconception of Lewin's work is that you are your behaviors. You're more than your behaviors (Ebbinghaus and Ruger 1855). Behaviorism as a psychological philosophy is pretty much dead; however, the perceived validity of behaviorism still lingers (Chomsky 1959).

Defining Boundaries

A moment ago, we sidestepped the issue that you are, in some sense, a different person if you violate a defining boundary. If you had a defining boundary that you wouldn't steal, and the circumstances forced you into a position where you did steal, it would cause a change in your personality.

> Once a defining boundary has been crossed, the person is forever changed.

The short-term impact of that situation might cause depression, anger, frustration, or a host of disruptive emotions. The longer-term impact is that you will become a different person. However, this is not to say that you have multiple selves; rather, your "self" changed. One could argue that this is like a state of matter change—like water turning to ice. You, for instance, changed only for the time where the circumstances drove you outside of your boundaries. However, in our experience, once a defining boundary has been crossed, the person is forever changed. A better analogy would be the change that happens when you fry an egg. It changed from a liquid to a solid permanently. It's not to say that the boundary might not be reestablished, but there will be a part of you that is forever changed by the experience.

The Partial Reveal

TV shows are famous for the partial reveal. Right before a break, they'll reveal part of what is to come. In doing this, they create interest for viewers to watch the commercials and a craving to see what the rest is (Duhigg 2012). The mechanisms work a bit differently for us when we only partially reveal ourselves to other people, but the result is the same. Others only get to see a part of us. They get to see only what we want them to see.

Our church friends wouldn't understand the drunken "debauchery" that happened on Saturday night. It wasn't *really* harmful. It was some old pals, and we were just having fun. We hadn't been able to cut up since that trip to Mardi Gras a few years ago. Come to think about it, they wouldn't approve of that trip either.

It's not like you can share with your friends how you're serving in the prison ministry and caring for men and women who have found themselves incarcerated. They wouldn't understand how you could be around "those people."

They may not understand, but that's not the real reason for not telling them. The real reason is that we don't believe they'd approve. We want—and, at some level, need—to be accepted. Because of that, we can't share parts of our lives that don't fit into the neatly defined box of what these friends expect of us.

So, we begin to fabricate partial images of ourselves. We figure out how to create illusions of the person we are. There's a different illusion for each of the groups that we interact with. The problem is that we eventually begin to believe that this projection is a version of our real self.

Difficulty of Projecting a False Image of Yourself

Projecting an image is hard. In the physics of projection, light falls off over the square of distance—that is, it's exponentially harder to project an image the further the projected image is from the source.

A more practical example might make more sense. Take a gallon jug of water or milk. If you can't find that, grab a five-pound bag of sugar, flour, potatoes or something that you can hold easily. Hold it next to your body at chest height. Do this for a minute or two.

For most people, this part of the exercise is very easy. We hold five pounds all the time. It's not taxing at all. Now, take the same object and hold it out to your side, keeping your arm fully extended and horizontal. Try to do this for a minute or two. Whether or not you keep the item to your side for the entire time, holding an item away from you is more strenuous than holding it close.

This is the same problem we have with our pro-jected selves. When we project an image that is more like who we really are, it's easier. When we try to project images that are radically different from our whole selves, we find it to be psychologically diffi-cult—even for short times.

> When we try to project images that are radically different from our whole selves, we find it to be psychologically difficult—even for short times.

We can see this when we attend events that don't fit who we really are. It could be a fancy gala, where we get the opportunity to dress up, but we're not exactly sure which fork to use or what should be said in "polite" conversation. Similarly, if you're not really the kind of person who likes sporting events, but you feel like you need to go out with friends to a game, you may find it's intensely stressful, as you're not sure how to project the kind of image that is expected in that situation. Projection may be necessary at times to ensure your acceptance, but it's exhausting to do continuously or even routinely.

Lack of Acceptance

In our need for acceptance, we believe—sometimes correctly—that if we reveal all of ourselves, we won't be accepted. Whatever the group or role is that we're filling won't accept the whole person that we are. So, we pro-tect ourselves by only revealing the parts of ourselves that we believe can be acceptable.

You probably have friends whose house or apartment you rarely went to. When you did visit, it was scheduled well in advance, and you got more than a slight impression that they had been cleaning their house all day. For the most part, you're probably not a judging person and wouldn't care much about how they keep house; but somewhere in their history, their mother said you can't have people over to your house unless it's clean.

The result is that they hide their poor housekeeping practices. They can't ask whether you care if their house is dirty or not, because that's not safe. Instead, they make sure to plan activities with you away from the house—even if that means spending more money. Instead of inviting you over for a simple meal prepared at home, they meet you out at a restaurant.

What about the friends who won't talk about their work? Most police officers won't talk about work. It's not that they'll clam up when you ask what they do, but if you ask about their day, they rarely are open enough to explain how they had to take a child from their parents. It's too complicated. There's too much internal conflict. They don't know how they feel, and they're worried that you'll label them as a monster or cruel. It's much, much easier to say little or nothing.

As a quick sidebar, if you have family members who can't talk about what they do, there are a few things you can do to help make it easier. First, don't judge what they do. They're doing their job. They trust that what they're doing is right, and they must do that to be able to survive. Second, ask questions that aren't sensitive. Ask how the mood in the office is or what they're going to do "with the guys" next. This is a safe opening for them to be able to speak without needing to be concerned about judgment. By asking questions like this, you can indicate your acceptance of them and make them feel heard, even if they can't talk about the core of their work.

INTEGRATED

With all the stress and energy necessary to maintain separate images, it may seem like having an integrated self-image is the easy answer. However, most folks find that having an integrated self-image isn't all it's cracked up to be.

Mismatches

One of the conveniences that having separate self-images allows for is having pieces of the overall puzzle that don't fit. After all, you don't have to worry that going out to the bar and being a faithful Muslim don't mesh if you don't ever try to get them to. If you keep them separate, you don't have to work so that they can fit together.

At work, you want to produce the image of a reliable worker who can be counted on to get things done no matter what. At home, you pride yourself in being available to family when they need you, whether that's a piano recital, a baseball game, or a PTO meeting. In integrating a self-image, you've got to navigate the clean and easy lines to find ways to make them work together.

You can't project the image that you're always there no matter what at the office and be the always-there PTO room parent. They're incompatible, and, at some level, you know it. You know that you can't have two top priorities. You must have a way to become clear about how you will make things work.

In this case, you might agree that you'll normally work your forty hours a week and occasionally a forty-five-hour week—but never more than once a month. You could further commit to make up time the same day in the evening if you have a school function—except for two days per year when you'll make yourself available for school field trips. You'll accept that there will be some evenings when you can't help your children do their homework because you helped make their party at school a reality last week and now you need to catch up on work.

While that all fits neatly into a package of a paragraph, we can tell you that getting to that sort of an understanding is not easy—and it's rare to get the boundaries and rules so clearly articulated. It also represents a simplification. In the example, we only dealt with PTO schedules and work. We didn't cover work travel for you or your spouse. We didn't cover when you should make exceptions—and when you shouldn't.

This is why building an integrated image is so hard. You must fix the places that there are conflicts, define the boundaries, and even put a framework for exceptions in place. With the complexities of life, this is fluid and frustratingly difficult. This isn't the hardest part of getting to an integrated self-image. Accepting the parts of ourselves that we don't like is harder.

The Bad, Too

When you're only looking at part of a picture, it's easy to focus on the good and ignore the bad. It's true that the dog's tail is blurry, but the rest of the composition is really good. However, when you get to an integrated image, you must look at the whole thing. As a result, you have to look at the pieces of yourself that you don't like.

We all have them, whether it's body image, our intellect, our finances, or our spiritual life. There is always something about us that we don't like, that we feel like we *need* to improve upon. It's easy to gloss over these things if we have multiple self-images but much more difficult if we want to get to one image.

There's the constant conflict between the person we want to be and the person we'd prefer to be. That is, being the kind of person that we want to be means that there are times when we must act, even when we'd prefer to pull the covers up over our head and stay in bed all day. It's hard to be the kind of person who believes in helping others if you're also the person who wants to lounge around every weekend.

Adulting

We call the process of resolving these conflicts "adulting." And, as is often said around our house by ourselves and our children, "adulting is hard." We often add, ". . . but the rewards are worth it." Resolving discrepancies between our images and our behaviors is difficult. Often it forces us to move from our ideals of who we are and what we believe to a more realistic view, and that means we're not really as good as we would love to believe we are.

> Resolving discrepancies between our images and our behaviors is difficult.

However, the reduced stress you feel from your day-to-day life is amazing. The ability to save energy going through each day leaves you feeling more energized. It's hard to explain what it's like to not have to cope with the burden of multiple self-images when you've never experienced it. It's sort of like the difference between not having glasses and having them. Before you ever have glasses or contacts, you believe the world is as you see it. You cope. After you get glasses, you get a clarity you never had—and the world, or at least seeing, is easier.

An integrated self-image doesn't change reality. It changes how you see reality.

CHAPTER SUMMARY

- Culture teaches us that we are "multiple" people: we are different people or have different images depending on where we are and who we are with.
- You are more than your behaviors or who you project yourself to be.
- Projecting an image that is not consistent with your self-image is exhausting, yet we may do this because we have a need to feel accepted. We may believe we will not be accepted if we are ourselves.
- Resolving the conflict between our images, our behaviors, and a more realistic view of ourselves is a difficult yet necessary step toward an integrated self-image.

DISCUSSION QUESTIONS

1. We all have multiple, sometimes competing, images; list a few images you maintain. Where do you project each image, and what is the group that you share it with?
2. Think about the above images and the instances you use each in. How do these images reflect your true self-image?
3. What are some tangible ways you can adjust your various images to a more integrated or realistic self-image?

Defining Your Goals

Most of the time, our goals are hidden in the shadows. We don't know exactly what we want or how to get there. Whether we're aware of what we want, where we're headed, or what our specific goals are, we are influenced by them. The clearer that we can get about what we want out of our current situation and our lives, the more resistant we'll make ourselves to burnout—and the clearer we can navigate a path out of burnout if we get there.

> The clearer that we can get about what we want out of our current situation and our lives, the more resistant we'll make ourselves to burnout.

GOALS AND VISIONS

Before diving into what our goals are personally, we should stop and explain what a goal is. It sounds obvious that a goal is something you want. However, there's a continuum between the very SMART goal and a goal that's a vision.

SMART Goals

SMART is an acronym:

- Specific
- Measurable
- Achievable
- Realistic
- Time-bound

These are the kind of goals that you'll find on your individual performance plan at an organization. They're the kinds of things that you measure a project against. Specific is good. They must be more or less directly measurable. At the end of the day, you want to be able to indicate, with a thumbs up or a thumbs down, whether the goal was met.

These aren't the kinds of goals we're talking about when we're talking about your personal goals. Personal goals can't be too specific, or you'll frustrate yourself. We can't know exactly how our world will turn out. Nor can we make the goals too intrinsically measurable. Bob Pozen, in his book

Extreme Productivity, explains that, while he tried to structure his world and work toward his goals, he was often directed as much by luck as by planning (Pozen 2012). Personal life goals aren't the kind of goals that are SMART. Instead, personal goals are more like a direction or a vision.

Visions

The opposite end of the spectrum from a SMART goal is a vision. It is like the difference between going to a specific address and simply heading west. With a goal, the specific target is well known. In the vision case, there is no specific target. There's just a way to get moving. Personal goals sit between these two extremes. They are specific enough to be somewhat measurable while remaining open-ended enough to allow for some variation.

The Middle Ground

Finding a middle ground that is both measurable and adaptable is important. If you're headed in a general direction, a road closure doesn't have much impact. If you're headed to a specific destination, a road closure could mean a substantial change. Life is going to have some road closures. We have to understand how to form our goals in such a way that neither the precise path nor the specific end time is so set in stone that we can't adapt to changes and challenges along the way.

Life is probabilistic, not deterministic (Rosenzweig 2007). That is, we can't say with certainty that any given thing will happen. We can only assess the probability that something will happen and work toward a goal. We can't say that we'll make it to work by 8:00 a.m. tomorrow; we can only say that we'll create the goal of doing it and will hope that conditions allow it. The more specific, or SMART, our goal is, the more we have to accept that circumstances may make this impossible.

Personal Goals

Ultimately, when thinking about our personal goals, we need to consider what we want in terms that are both broad enough to allow for the variations in life and specific and measurable enough to know whether we've accomplished them.

We also need to consider that, when we set our goals, they should generally be set without a stopping rule. That is, we don't want to set our goal to play at Carnegie Hall. We want to be the best musician possible, so that playing at Carnegie Hall is a reasonably expected outcome. The reason we don't want a specific end goal is that the sudden accomplishment of a personal life goal often leaves people disoriented. You become vulnerable to burnout because you're no longer making progress toward a goal, and, for a brief period, you may not have another one. This can create a spiral that traps you into helplessness.

Another consideration for personal goals is that you shouldn't have just one goal. Despite others' guidance that you have a single goal, it's safer to have a set of goals for different areas for your life. Should you become temporarily stuck in one area of your life, you can still see progress in other areas (Keller and Papasan 2013). It's natural to be blocked from moving toward your personal goals from time to time. Resilience comes from recognizing that you're making progress toward at least one goal even if you're blocked in other areas.

> Resilience comes from recognizing that you're making progress toward at least one goal even if you're blocked in other areas.

CREATING GOALS

Clayton Christensen has a pointed way of asking, "How will you measure your life?" in the title of his book (Christensen, Allworth, and Dillon 2012). This question is the right question. If you imagine yourself at the end of your life, when you're sitting comfortably and chatting with a good friend about what you're proudest of in your life, what do you say?

Bronnie Ware tackles the opposite approach in *The Top Five Regrets of the Dying*. In it, she records the five regrets she heard most as a palliative care nurse (Ware 2011):

1. I wish I had the courage to live a life true to myself, not the life others expected of me.
2. I wish I hadn't worked so hard.
3. I wish I had the courage to express my feelings.

4. I wish I had stayed in touch with my friends.
5. I wish I had let myself be happier.

It's important to realize that these regrets are often the opposite of the goals that they may have had for themselves—to live life wholeheartedly, to enjoy life, and to be more connected with others. Adam Grant, in *Originals*, shares that other people regret the things they didn't do more than they appreciate the things that they did (Grant 2016).

These are the generic answers that apply to everyone. How do we make them specific to the things that are important to each of us individually? While these provide a framework for the kinds of goals we want to consider, we each need to individually make our own list.

Bucket Lists

The exercise of considering what you would be most proud of isn't saying the things that you want on your bucket list. A bucket list—if you're unfamiliar with the phrase—is the list of things that you want to do before you die. However, these are most frequently expressed as the things you want to try or the places you want to go. They can be what you want to accomplish, but they rarely are.

Bucket lists tend to be very personal lists, and while they're not personal life goals in themselves, they may be in aggregate. For instance, we, the authors, have a goal of seeing all the lighthouses in the United States. The beauty of this bucket list item is that it's flexible. First, what do we do about the lighthouses that are on islands? We've seen some of them, but do we rent a boat to see them all? Similarly, if we manage to see all the lighthouses in the United States, do we extend our goal to include the lighthouses of Canada as well?

We'd encourage you to create—and keep updating—your personal bucket list. You can remove things if you decide they're not worth the effort and add things as you become more interested in them. This exercise isn't about what you can check off a list. The exercise is about being open to understanding what's interesting or important to you. While the specific tasks that you want to accomplish may not reveal much about you any more than knowing we want to see lighthouses tells you about us, the process connects you with what matters to you, and it can be instructive in that way.

Eulogy

Another way to think about what your goals should be—one that is only slightly more morbid—is to imagine what would you want said about you in your eulogy. If your best friend, your wife, or your children were to stand up and tell the world the things that they think most embody you or were your greatest accomplishments, what would they say?

You'll find that these are rarely the specific goals that might happen. Playing at Carnegie Hall likely won't make the list. Nor will seeing all the lighthouses in the United States. Everyone at the service will already know that. What will tend to make the list are the enduring characteristics. They might be the boundless compassion, the unending charity. It might be the hunger for learning or the disdain for systems that cause people harm. Whatever it is that you would like said about you, those are your hidden goals for who you want to be.

Converting an enduring characteristic into a path that you can walk with more specific goals isn't always easy, but at least you know the direction you're headed.

From Death to Life

There's no doubt that the preceding exercises can be morbid. However, completing these exercises is the only reliable way that we've found to get folks to confront their mortality long enough to discover what is important. The mental journey to the end of your life was only to make clear what's important in the end. How, then, do we convert this learning to what to do during our lives to leave us with happiness and fulfillment?

WHY?

Simon Sinek suggests that, in any activity, you should "start with why" (Sinek 2009) to inspire people. Instead of telling them what to do, you should tell them why it's important. However, rarely do we tell ourselves, or bother to discover, why we want to do something. "Why" can be a powerful question, especially if asked repeatedly—but not like a young toddler.

Means and Ends

The power of why is in helping you to discover what you really want and what is just a means to an end. The separation of means and ends (which is an end in and of itself) goes all the way back to Aristotle's *Nicomachean Ethics.* Simply put, "means" are things we do or want in order to get something else, which is an "end."

For instance, we don't generally want a job because we want the job itself. More likely we want the things that the job will bring to us, like money or status. We don't want a dog for the sake of owning a dog. We want the dog because we want a companion, or we want something furry to cuddle with. Frequently, when we look deeply at what we say we want, we'll find that it's not the "thing" we want, but what we believe the thing will lead us to.

Care should be exercised here, because sometimes one person's ends is another person's means. Someone can want a car as a means of transportation, or they can want a car just because they want it. There's no hard-and-fast rule about what is a means and what is an end in and of itself. We must ferret out which is which, and that is done by asking why.

The Five Whys

One way of getting to the heart of the matter, moving past the goals that are merely means to an end, is to continue asking why. Typically, in a root cause analysis, this is done five times. The approach can feel repetitive and frustrating, like answering an incessant toddler; however, done with the right frame of mind, it can move you from means to means—and finally to an end.

The five whys persist even when given a seemingly final answer because sometimes there are more deeply held desires that sit below the instrumental desires we're aware of. We may not want the car for transportation, but instead it may be a way of indicating status to others.

DEALING WITH MISALIGNMENT

What happens when your goals and the goals of those around you, particularly at work, don't align, and what should you do about it? In simple terms, any substantial degree of misalignment will create a propensity toward burnout. You will not perceive support for your goals, you may see poor results, and it may be difficult to accomplish self-care in an environment that doesn't value what you value. As a result, you effectively have two solutions. First, you can bring the goals into better alignment. Second, you can seek other opportunities.

Bringing Goals into Alignment

In getting things into alignment, you also have two options. You can move the company goals, or you can move your goals. You must change one or the other position to accomplish the goal of bringing them into better alignment. Neither is going to be easy, but both are possible.

Most organizations operate without a clear understanding of their core defining goals and what they believe. Further, these goals operate differently in different departments. This lack of definition and these inconsistencies create opportunities. If your organization has a well-articulated, understood, and consistent set of goals, the ability to move them is severely limited. It's hard to change the goals of an organization that has fought to well define those goals.

> It's possible to shift your short-term or temporary goals toward learning more about yourself, an industry, or a skill in service to your ultimate goal.

Changing your own goals may seem easier than changing the goals of an organization, but changing your deeply rooted goals may be difficult. It's more likely that you'll be able to adjust your temporary goals if they don't oppose the organizational goals. It's possible to shift your short-term or temporary goals toward learning more about yourself, an industry, or a skill in service to your ultimate goal. This temporary adjustment may be enough to keep you out of burnout for a while as you develop what you need to reach your end goals.

Finding a Place with Alignment

Whether you can't adjust either goal and find the misalignment too great, or you've exhausted your capacity to stay with your adjusted goals, there are times that finding opportunities outside the organization is the appropriate answer. The biggest challenge with finding a new place with better alignment to your goals is that often the espoused beliefs and the actual beliefs of an organization don't match. You'll need to do more than sit in an interview for an hour to know whether they're the right fit or not. It will take some keen observation and some tough questions.

If you're looking to find the right place, you may want to ask questions like:

1. Tell me about one time when your values were tested, and what did you do to resolve the situation?
2. What do you feel was the greatest challenge that the department or the organization has faced in the last five years?

These sorts of questions force the organization to discuss those difficult spots in their history. You'll need to be prepared for long and nuanced answers—which can help you understand whether the goals and beliefs of the organization are aligned with yours.

CHAPTER SUMMARY

- Identifying what we want out of our current situation and our life will help develop resistance to burnout.
- Goals can range from very detailed, SMART goals to a somewhat fuzzy vision.
- We need to develop personal goals that are broad enough to allow for the variations in life and specific and measurable enough to know whether we are achieving them.
- Multiple goals over various areas of your life without specific stopping points provide opportunities to continue moving toward your goals without becoming stuck or goalless.
- Considering what you want to be known or remembered for can be a framework for developing goals.
- A bucket list of things you want to do is different from personal goals. A bucket list can assist in being open and understanding what is interesting or important to you.

- When considering a goal, it is useful to ask why it is important. In this way, you can sort through the means and find the end reason something is important.
- Situations where your personal goals and organizational goals are in alignment are resistant to burnout and provide the support to meet your personal goals.

DISCUSSION QUESTIONS

1. What are the three primary areas of your life? (Areas may include work, family, social, sports, personal, etc.)
2. Pick one area of your life and list three goals for that area. Remember to keep the goals broad enough to allow for variation while still being measurable.
3. For each of the goals that you have developed, work through a series of five whys to better understand what it is that you truly desire.
4. Consider how your goals are aligned with your world. If they are not aligned, how can you better bring them into alignment?

CHAPTER 14

Motivation and Meaning

The most common symptom of burnout, the one that leads everyone to question what is going on, is a lack of motivation. Burned-out people wake up and wonder why they're pushing so hard to do so many things, and they feel like they're not getting anywhere. It's like walking through muck every day with no end in sight. By learning what motivates us, we can learn how to motivate ourselves. We can learn what it takes to keep moving forward—no matter how slowly—in the face of the pressures of day-to-day life.

> By learning what motivates us, we can learn how to motivate ourselves.

In this chapter, we'll also explore beyond the motivation to the meaning and purpose that pulls us forward and makes us decide that the struggle is worth the effort, whether we succeed or not.

MOTIVATION

What makes people want to do something? Motivation is a tricky thing. It changes and adapts. It can be manipulated subtly. Throughout our history, we've seen two models of motivation come and go, and we've entered into a time when our personal motivations seem to be formed by our creative nature. Let's quickly review the biological theory of motivation, the carrots and sticks model, and finally settle on the creative model.

Biological Motivation

Anyone who has had a high school education has probably heard of Maslow's hierarchy of needs. It's a model that Maslow used to describe how animals focus their energies toward their most urgent needs and move to higher levels only after those basic needs are met.

At the lowest levels, it's about physiological needs like food and water. As it moves up, it speaks about the need for safety and further up comes love and belonging. The two highest levels are esteem and self-actualization. As models go, it's useful but also incomplete. People don't always pursue these in the order of the hierarchy.

The key challenge is the proverbial starving artist who foregoes physiological needs—or at least their safety needs—in the service of their self-actualization needs. An artist friend of ours says that, in truth, artists aren't literally starving—however, at the very least, they're forgoing some of their safety needs.

Carrots and Sticks Motivation

While Maslow's hierarchy of needs may be interesting, it doesn't truly say much about how employers and other people can motivate you—or how you can motivate other people. For that, we need the works of Pavlov and his dogs. Pavlov, as you probably also learned in high school, conditioned dogs to salivate at the sound of a bell by always ringing the bell before feeding the dogs. This class experiment forms the basis of a motivational model called classical conditioning, which involves involuntary responses associated with certain stimuli. You expect that, if something occurs or you perform an action, there will be a result, whether you have control of the stimulus or not. Paired with the later concept of operant conditioning, which is the voluntary training of behavior, this amounts to rewards and punishments, or "carrots and sticks."

When the animal—or human—does something that you want, you reward them. When they do something you don't want, you punish them. In zoology, a variant of operant conditioning only uses rewards and no punishments. This is frequently done with wild animals that are far too powerful and unpredictable to punish.

The model forms the basis of historical methods of management. The employees were kept in line through a series of rewards and punishments. It's still an effective way to shape the character of children. However, it has lost its efficacy with adults.

Some folks practice a form of rewards and punishments on themselves, which tends to be similarly ineffective. It's much more effective to be compassionate and forgiving with yourself than it is to attempt to punish yourself.

Creative Motivation

Back in 2002, Richard Florida, in *The Rise of the Creative Class,* estimated that 30 percent of our economy was driven by what he calls the "creative" class (Florida 2011). The creative class works differently from the way that people used to work. These folks, who worked in manufacturing, farming, and other professions, Florida calls the "working" class. There's also the new emergence of the "service" class, who work in service of others. Motivationally, the working and service classes seem similar. Their work is algorithmic. In other words, you do a series of steps, and you get a relatively predictable result. The creative class is different and heuristic. There's no one way to make a good book, painting, or piece of music. This takes a different kind of motivation.

Daniel Pink writes about this different kind of motivation in *Drive* (Pink 2011). Drawing on the work of others, he explains how motivation in a world of heuristic workers means something different. The differences are in three key aspects: autonomy, mastery, and purpose.

Autonomy

The ability to find our own way, it turns out, is one of the keys when there are many ways to get to the end goal. Autonomy is simply not having to work following the specific and detailed instructions of someone else. Instead, you're given a direction for where to go—but not how to do it. Sure, there's support if you need or want it, but, by and large, you're expected to deliver the result, not follow step-by-step instructions.

In the 1980s, one of the most regimented, structured, and autocratic organizations on the planet—the US Army—recognized the wisdom of the statement "no plan survives contact with the enemy." They moved from only specific instructions to specific instructions *and* the commander's intent (Heath and Heath 2007). The commander's intent is what the troops were to aim for if the plan didn't work, well, as planned.

Autonomy—or at least limited autonomy—has pervaded even the most unlikely of places because it's necessary to be motivated and adaptable for changing circumstances.

Mastery

Our ego is really an amazing thing. According to one tome, *The Ego and Its Defenses,* it has twenty-two major and twenty-six minor defenses (Laughlin 1970). Our ego wants us to be good at what we do. Though there are many defenses in the arsenal, our ego much prefers that its defenses not be needed. Our ego drives us toward the belief that we're better than others. That's why only 2 percent of high school seniors believe their leadership skills are below average, and a full 25 percent of people believe they're in the top 1 percent in their ability to get along with others (Heath and Heath 2010).

Our desire, then, is to become masters of whatever we do. We want to become the best. We may not be willing to put in the ten thousand hours that it takes to become a true master at something, but we want to achieve mastery nonetheless (Gladwell 2008). While ten thousand hours may not be the exact number, the dedication and purposeful practice is a great deal of work and commitment (Ericsson and Pool 2016).

Despite the barriers to mastery, we all want to feel successful, that we're good at what we're doing. Even with all the ego's defenses, it can't always help us feel that way. Therefore, creating the perceptions that we are masters—or at least on the path of mastery—is a key component of motivating people, including ourselves.

Purpose

Largely, the struggle for survival is gone. Viktor Frankl's experience in the Nazi concentration camps brought him face-to-face with a struggle for survival of another kind. His response to that tragedy was a work with the English title *Man's Search for Meaning* (Frankl 1959). His observation was that those persons who had meaning—even modest meaning—survived, and those who didn't have purpose did not. Half a century later, Atul Gawande, a brilliant surgeon and author, wrote about his quest to find a place of dignity for his aging parents in *Being Mortal* (Gawande 2014). Gawande discovered that when residents were given small things to take care of, they survived longer and appeared more active and alert.

Purpose is a powerful component of our motivation that means the difference between life and death, but the purpose that we hold can be tiny and seemingly insignificant. Whether reducing the suffering of other inmates or taking care of a plant, the desire is enough to mean the difference between being motivated to live or allowing death.

When we speak about finding purpose to build motivation, we're not necessarily speaking about ridding the world of hunger or curing cancer. Humble purposes seem to be as effective as large ones.

Your purpose may be caring for or providing for your family. It may be to help members of your community. Anything that gives your life meaning—to you—is enough.

MEANING

Philosophers have sought the universal meaning of life since the beginning of time, and the best answer that anyone has come up with—in jest—is "42." The answer 42 comes from *The Hitchhiker's Guide to the Galaxy* (Adams 1979). In Adams's classic, the answer doesn't have a specific question. The point is that when a question is not asked well, the answer you get may be useless. That's part of the challenge in defining meaning. How is our meaning—or purpose—being considered? In our context, we can, luckily, frame our discussion to personal meaning. When we find a meaning that works for us, we don't have to be concerned if it's the same meaning as others around us.

Figuring out meaning is both deeply personal and fluid. Rob thought that the meaning of his life would be to raise a family, but for a time that felt unobtainable. He then thought that the meaning of his life would be to make complicated topics easier for other people to understand. However, when he and Terri met and married, that changed, too. Meaning became about preventing healthcare-associated infections (HAIs). This book—at least for his part—is about HAIs and education. Research indicates that burnout is correlated with higher HAI rates.

Along the way, there have been many related things that we, the authors, have done, from child-safety playing cards to programs designed to help teens learn how to better cope with the world (AvailTek LLC 2018). Nothing that we do is exactly aligned with our precise meaning at that moment, but ideally, the things that we're doing are generally aligned in the right direction.

The Compass and the Map

When you're trying to find your meaning in life, you're trying to find your way. In everyday spatial terms, the way we navigate is with GPSs, compasses, and maps. In today's age of GPS technology, few folks rely on old-fashioned maps and compasses any longer. The technology is reliable and doesn't require batteries, but fewer people recognize the value of both. A printed-on-paper map doesn't tell you where you are, nor does a compass. However, all together, a compass, a map, and a bit of work can tell you where you are and help get you where you want to go.

The compass can't tell you where you are, but it can tell you where you are headed. Your meaning is where you are headed. It's the compass that points the way to where you want to go. Having that ever-present needle orienting you provides just enough context to see your way.

> Your meaning is where you are headed. It's the compass that points the way to where you want to go.

While a map isn't the territory, it is a smaller representation of that territory that you can use to orient yourself. Unlike GPS receivers with maps, it can't tell you where you are. A map can, however, communicate features that you can use to help identify where you are. Look for the tall mountains or the big lake and compare that to what you see to discover your location. Cartography (mapmaking) is an art form that helps to focus the things on the map to the things that you can use to orient yourself.

When trying to find—and define—our meaning, we must identify the topology of our world to define what constitutes the right direction and which way is wrong. We must identify which reference points we're going to use. Are we going to measure ourselves against our neighbors or our mentors?

The challenge with a map is that it takes a long time to be certain that you're in the spot you believe you're in. You need to be able to verify the landscape changes as you would expect it to as you move in a direction. It's a relatively common situation to believe you're in one place only to realize you're in a completely different place. Perhaps the most famous case of this is Columbus's discovery of the "new world," but it happens on a much smaller scale every day.

When we're navigating the map of the meaning in our world, we must move in a direction and see that the things we believe are important are getting closer and those that aren't important are getting further away.

Tacking into the Wind

Sometimes the way that you want to go—the way you think your meaning is pulling you—may be the way you're being pushed away from by life's circumstances. You may believe that your mission is to help others when the world is telling you to take advantage of others. It may be that your real goal is to help people learn, but you find that you're not reaching enough people. When you find the wind in your face, you can learn from sailing.

Most folks understand how to sail a boat when the wind is at your back. You put the sails up and you're pushed along. However, few people—except sailors—have considered how you move into the wind. That is, how can you move toward the wind when it's in your face? The answer is to tack into the wind. It's the manipulation of the sails and the rudder, so that you're pointing slightly off-angle from where the wind is coming from. You're generally angled toward the wind, but the shape of the sail and direction of the boat still capture the wind and use it to propel you forward. In sailing, you tack left then right (technically port then starboard) to keep from getting too far off course in any one direction. It's not as easy as sailing with the wind to your back, but it's definitely possible to make progress, even when the wind is in your face.

> For most of us, life is like tacking into the wind.

For most of us, life is like tacking into the wind. We can't directly reach our goal. We have to shoot a bit right of our target, then a bit left. We may not even know where things will end up when we start. We may find that we're starting with just the general idea of the right place.

Approximately OK

When it comes to finding your meaning, approximately right or approximately OK is the best you're going to do. Our meanings move. Our world changes. Our understanding changes. Our goal with defining a meaning is to put something out there where we can manage the gap between where we want to go and where we are. We want to create a level of desire that is neither too much nor too little. Finding your personal meaning may be more than what can be accomplished in a few pages—but at least now you can start to define your meaning, recognizing that you don't have to get it exactly right. You can move closer even when the wind is in your face.

CHAPTER SUMMARY

- A lack of motivation is the most common symptom of burnout.
- Motivation is frequently thought to be based on needs, rewards, or punishments. These motivators are rarely the most effective for adults.
- Autonomy, mastery, and purpose are effective motivators for adults. We want to have input on solutions, be effective at (or master) our work, and have meaning in the world.
- Finding your personal meaning, no matter how grand or humble, provides motivation and resilience to burnout.
- Personal meaning is not a destination. It is a direction that allows you to move from where you are today to where you want to be.
- Your personal meaning may change over time, but the goal is to create a desire that is not overwhelming nor uninspiring.

DISCUSSION QUESTIONS

1. Consider your top three to five things that motivate you. Are they things, feelings, rewards, or accomplishments?
2. Our purpose or personal meaning can be a key motivator that guides life. How would you define your personal meaning or purpose? Identify at least one purpose to ponder and form into your current (malleable) personal meaning.
3. Continue pondering the personal meaning you have developed over the next few days and weeks. As you experience life and "tack into the wind," feel the support of your purpose helping you to move toward your goals.

CHAPTER 15

Internal Barriers to Efficacy

Sometimes the barriers we face aren't external barriers; they are barriers that we carry on the inside. We feel like we can't get something done, not because of an external condition or circumstance but because, deep down inside, we're stuck. Internal barriers are often harder to deal with than external barriers because they're harder to see.

In this chapter, we will look at the internal barriers that feed burnout, the ways to identify what they are, and steps to take to move beyond them.

WHAT ARE BARRIERS?

A barrier is frequently defined as "a circumstance or obstacle that keeps people or things apart or prevents communication or progress." Internal barriers are those beliefs and self-imposed limits that keep us from achieving our goals. These barriers can hold us hostage. The biggest challenge with these internal barriers is that they are so integrated into our beliefs that we do not even recognize that they are there, nor do we ever imagine that it is possible to move beyond them.

> Internal barriers are those beliefs and self-imposed limits that keep us from achieving our goals.

There are two kinds of barriers that many of us struggle with: "the story of never" and "stories in our voices."

The Story of Never

While Rob and Terri, the authors, were on a trip to Maine to look at lighthouses and share some quiet time together, Terri shared that she had wanted to go to Maine for as long as she could remember, yet she never believed she would get to go. As they were talking, Rob shared that he never doubted that he could go to Maine sometime. The more they talked, the more they recognized that believing something can never happen so limits our beliefs that it prevents us from trying at all.

Even as they started the trip, her "never" did not go completely away. While literally in Maine, she was still thinking that she'd never get to go. The "never" was so strong that it overpowered the actual reality. Rob, having overheard that Terri wanted to see the whales and having listened to all the reasons she made up as to why they couldn't, pointed the car toward Bar

Harbor, where the whale-watching boats left. Once they were there and had their tickets, her "never" finally was put to rest. There were many pieces to the belief in her "never." Most of them were based on someone else's thoughts and then well fed by her imagination over time.

Neither Rob nor Terri have a history of planning trips and not going, nor do they agree they want to do something and then back out of it. She could trust that, when they made plans, they would follow through. The "never" was really just in her head. The problem is that it was also far enough from her conscious thought that she could not see it or identify it. After their trip, a friend from high school remarked that she really enjoyed the pictures, because she would probably "never" get to go. That resonated. It's real how many people struggle with the story that something will never happen. Terri still has the tickets for the whale watch in her wallet to remind her that what may seem impossible is really possible.

Perhaps there are "nevers" that you're holding on to that you're not even aware of.

Stories in Our Voices

Our internal barriers come from somewhere. In most cases, it's because someone in our past told us that the barrier existed. They set our expectations about what could, should, couldn't, and shouldn't be a part of our lives. We've internalized these beliefs and now hear them in our own heads, but in our voice, not someone else's. We believe our voice tells us the truth, even when it doesn't. Slyly, these voices have become ours even though they're not true. We may hear, "You have to do this to be a good parent or spouse or worker," or, "You can't, you just are not enough." These limiting thoughts are unwelcome gifts from those we have known in our lives and can become seemingly insurmountable barriers—if we can even see that they're there.

Just like the story of never, these voices are persistent and difficult to shake loose. The only way to confront something that seems to be truth is with other—real—truth. We have to find aspects of the voices that are verifiably untrue. If the voice tells you that you're unlovable, you confront it not with others' words about how they love you but with the things that they've done to demonstrate their love. When confronted with such evidence, the voices are reluctantly forced to change what they're saying.

If you hear that "you'll never amount to anything," you can confront that with your successes. Whether it's winning a spelling bee, getting first place in a three-legged race, or something more important to you, confront the voice with something that cannot be challenged. The first defense of these voices will be to minimize the facts that you leverage in the argument. Stand your ground. If the word is you'll never amount to anything, then anything you do amount to is, well, something.

IDENTIFYING BARRIERS

As we mentioned, internal barriers are incredibly hard to identify. However, it can be done. Let's take a look at some common barriers and what we can do to find them, so we can remove them.

Fear

We all have fears. In fact, fear can take over our lives to the point that we sometimes forget what it is like to live without it (Warrell 2009). Fear can become such a barrier that we lose not only the ability to be effective but also the ability to create the life we desire. There are a multitude of things we may fear, from failing to succeeding and almost every step in between.

The best way to identify our fears is to listen to our bodies and to feel that little spark of discomfort as we approach something. Rather than suppressing the feeling, we can pause and wonder why the spark occurred. From this thought, we can explore what is going on and begin to ask why.

Identity

Too often, our identity is fragmented and disconnected, as we discussed in the chapter on integrated self-image. Each of us is unique, important, and amazing in our own right, but this is often lost in the hurry of our daily routine. Developing a complete, realistic self-awareness takes time and energy, but the outcome of this activity is one of the biggest gifts we can give to ourselves (Freudenberger and Richelson 1981).

A failure to accept or acknowledge a component of our true nature can be a major barrier to our happiness and success in life. A lack of clarity on who we are—including what we will and will not do—can keep us from achieving our goals. If you're not sure who you are, and you believe that's preventing you from success, try practicing some of the tips we suggested in the integrated self-image chapter.

Responsibility

Sometimes it feels like we are responsible for the entire world. We may feel responsible for our children and their behavior, our parents, our spouse, our friends, our projects, our coworkers and their projects, and even our business. When our family does not act the way we taught them or the way we think they should act, we feel responsible. When our spouse says something to friends that embarrasses us, we feel responsible. The project is out of control, and we feel responsible. We feel responsible for a multitude of people and events around us.

The truth is that we cannot be responsible for what we cannot control. Each of us only controls a small set of items, including our behaviors, our reactions, and our actions.

When we try to take responsibility for others, we place massive and unrealistic demands upon ourselves. We can help avoid burnout by eliminating this unnecessary and unhealthy demand. We can identify our desire to take unnecessary responsibility by asking ourselves whether we have control of—or only influence over—the outcome. Unless we have control, we shouldn't hold ourselves responsible.

> We can identify our desire to take unnecessary responsibility by asking ourselves whether we have control of—or only influence over—the outcome.

Being Content

When you struggle to move a thousand goals on a thousand different fronts forward, you're almost certainly going to spread yourself too thin. You can't take on the world and expect to win. The secret to keeping focused on a few goals is to develop a sense of contentment about things that you're not willing or able to work on currently.

Almost all of us would love to have a healthier body, a bigger house, a better car, more exotic vacations, a better career, and so on. However, while we can do any of these, we can't do all of these at the same time. To be able to focus our energies toward specific goals, we have to accept and be content with things the way they are—until we're ready to tackle them. For some, that may mean staying in a job that isn't perfect while you're focused on developing children of character. For others, it means longer nights at the office instead of spending an hour at the gym.

Being content in some areas of our life, and not expecting to have everything, leads us toward success in the few things that we are able to focus on.

BREAKING BARRIERS

Once we start to recognize the barriers we carry in our heads, we can start to compare them to the reality around us. It is possible for Terri to believe that she cannot be a good wife and mother or that she cannot help people prevent healthcare-associated infections. She may even consider what is the most important to her and give up the rest because fear prevents her from believing she can be successful. If she takes the time to consider the truth, she can look at her children and realize that she has been and is a good mom. Her husband frequently reminds her that she is a good wife (even though it is his opinion here that matters, it is still sometimes hard to believe). Then she considers the work she has done and continues to do. The facts support that the beliefs in her head are wrong. Recognizing that the beliefs we hold about ourselves can actually be lies enables us to begin to remove the barriers and move beyond them.

> Recognizing that the beliefs we hold about ourselves can actually be lies enables us to begin to remove the barriers and move beyond them.

It takes diligence and practice to recognize the barriers in your head and look at reality to compare the two. You have to learn to hear the voice and compare the message with what you have experienced and learned to be truth. When you start looking at the truth, the barriers you carry in your head start to evaporate, and you find yourself able to achieve more than you expected.

Once we know who we are—when we discover our identity—we get to decide what we are going to believe and what we are going to cast aside. It is not an easy process, but it does lead us to a more peaceful existence and a realistic vision of where we can go.

MOST THINGS WE WANT ARE POSSIBLE

We know we cannot achieve everything we would like to achieve. However, removing the internal barriers that convince us we cannot do something allows us the chance to achieve those things that we want to.

Sir Edmond Hillary, the first man to reach the top of Mt. Everest, tells us that it is not the mountain that we conquer, but ourselves. Our purpose will be most rewarding when our goals fit well with who we are (Zachary 2015). We can move beyond who we believe ourselves to be and toward becoming the person we want to be by keeping our expectations realistic. We must first overcome our internal barriers; then we can move forward to greater perceived personal efficacy.

CHAPTER SUMMARY

- Barriers may be external or internal; both can prevent us from achieving our goals.
- Internal barriers may take different forms; they may be deeply held yet unconscious beliefs, or they may be echoes of barriers someone once told us we should have.
- The voices in our heads can tell us that we are not enough. We can use examples of the truth to combat these voices and eliminate the internal barriers they cause.
- Common internal barriers include fear, identity, responsibility, and contentment.
- You cannot be responsible for what you cannot control. This includes projects, family members, and all other aspects of life. Integrating this knowledge can change your life.
- Identifying the barriers in your head and comparing them to the reality around us is an effective step in removing the internal barriers that prevent us from reaching our goals.

DISCUSSION QUESTIONS

1. Consider the things you think about that may be internal barriers. List a barrier for your primary life areas (i.e., family, work, social).

2. For each of the internal barriers you identified, compare your thoughts to the actions or reality of the world around you, and think about how this reality may change your self-perspective. In what ways does reality validate or invalidate your beliefs?

3. Identify a few circumstances where you take responsibility for things that you cannot control. If you were to release yourself from this responsibility, how might this change your perspective?

CHAPTER 16

Resistance and Resilience

In *Star Trek: The Next Generation,* one of the "enemies" was the Borg, whose catchphrase was "Resistance is futile." The problem is that resistance isn't futile. Resistance is a part of the human condition and something that can be cultivated.

What's more powerful than resistance is resilience. Resilience is a centering or rooting in who you are, what you believe, and how you'll behave that allows you to avoid burnout almost passively. Instead of defending against burnout sneaking up on you, you'll learn to operate in ways that make it harder for burnout to take hold of you.

We start the conversation about resilience in this chapter and continue it through the rest of the book. Each chapter will give you a few more tools to add to your toolbox to prevent burnout or recover from it. Ultimately, when your toolbox is filled, you should be able to step out of burnout as easily as you would cross the threshold of a room.

RESISTANCE

All of us have seen signs of burnout in ourselves. Resistance is not denying that the signs are present; instead, it is confronting them and doing something about them. Resistance is taking an active stance toward protecting ourselves from entering burnout. We do this by intentionally and actively filling our personal agency.

Forced Filling

It's not always possible to directly manage your perception of your efficacy. Sometimes we fall back to the simpler model where we look for ways to fill up our personal agency bathtub by increasing our results, support, or self-care—and force our personal agency to increase.

Recognizing Results

Results aren't things that you can force to happen. However, you can change how you perceive the results. You can linger on the positive results that you see. You can visualize the people you've helped and keep close at hand any awards or rewards that you've received. Rick Hansen in *Hardwiring Happiness* provides many techniques for focusing more on the positive than the negative (Hanson 2013).

Soliciting Support

One of the things that many people who have recovered from burnout report is that they had much more support available to them than they realized. When they encounter feelings of burnout now, they're much more likely to reach out and ask for help and support rather than isolate themselves. You can't get support out of thin air, but it's amazing how people may be willing to help you if you only ask.

Strong Self-Care

As was mentioned in the first section, the most powerful way to fill up your personal agency is to spend more time on self-care. Understanding that self-care is really the most compassionate thing you can do for others and prioritizing it so that you have the reserves you need can make you virtually immune to burnout. In fact, the central characteristic of those with resilience is that they prioritize—and actually do—self-care.

RESILIENCE

Whereas resistance is active and relies on detecting the initial signs of burnout, resilience is a passive state of being able to weather the storms of life. Where resistance comes from vigilance and keeping an eye on signs for burnout, resilience comes from knowing and accepting who you are and the reality that surrounds us. Rick Hanson in *Resilient* says, "True resilience fosters well-being, an underlying sense of happiness, love, and peace" (Hanson 2018).

You've already developed a great deal of resilience as it comes to burnout through your understanding of how burnout works and how it can be addressed. The understanding makes it easier for you to know when things aren't right—when you've lost your center. You've also learned about goals, purpose, and meaning. The clearer you become on these items, the less likely you are to fall off into the pit of burnout. We'll address what it's like to have a stable core and how that allows you to remain centered. Then we will discuss the need for more than one anchor and how this helps you to stay rooted even when it feels like part of your world is falling apart. The rest of the book will speak to additional resilience techniques like cultivating hope, understanding failure, and developing detachment.

Centering with a Stable Core

> Having a stable core is about knowing who you are, what you believe, and where your boundaries are.

Having a stable core is about knowing who you are, what you believe, and where your boundaries are. While we've discussed each of these components already, it's time to bring them together to show how they fit and how they create a stable core that makes it hard for people to move you from your center.

Knowing who you are—and who you are not—starts with boundaries. Boundaries, as you recall, are the dividing line between me and "not me." They insulate us from people trying to inflict their beliefs and values on us. Boundaries are the mechanisms by which we can decide what we're going to let in and what must stay on the outside.

Beliefs, or values, are the lens that you use to create and revise your boundaries. Belief systems vary. Some people believe that eating meat is wrong (vegetarians), and others believe that eating anything that comes from an animal is wrong (vegans). Values aren't universal across all humans. Your unique set of values and, particularly, their relationship to other values helps to make you unique.

Your complete set of beliefs and boundaries—which lead to your behaviors—make you who you are. The process of finding your center or stable core is necessary to discover these values and boundaries and clearly and dispassionately articulate them.

Personality Tests

One way to try to discover your beliefs and boundaries is to take a set of personality profiling tests. Some of these tests are not useful in determining your values, but some, like the Values in Action (VIA) test, can help clarify what is and isn't important to you. You'll find the VIA test available for free at http://www.authentichappiness.org. Other tests, like the Enneagram and the Myers-Briggs Type Indicator (MBTI), also have free variants available online. By leveraging personality tests, you can sometimes become aware of things that are important to you that you've never realized.

Dynamic Anchors

We've recommended that you think about having a set of goals or objectives. The idea is that if you get stuck in one area of your life or on one goal, you can focus on another area until you become unblocked on the first. This approach allows you to be more in flow with the way that the world functions and accept timing that may not be your own. One of the most difficult things to realize is that it may be possible to tack into the wind—but it may be that it's easier and less exhausting to wait until the winds change. Similarly, we recommend that you don't define yourself with a single anchor.

Some people define themselves by one thing. It could be that they're a CEO, a rock star, or a stay-at-home mom. Whatever it is, this is the only portion of their identity. In identifying an integrated self-image, you define multiple aspects and facts about yourself, all of which fit together. Each of these self-images has a reference point. It's an anchor that represents what you think the ideal of these self-images should be. Each of these is an individual anchor for an aspect of your integrated self-image.

> Having an integrated self-image is an important point of building resilience because it allows you to leverage multiple anchors for stability and measurement.

Having an integrated self-image is an important point of building resilience because it allows you to leverage multiple anchors for stability and measurement. Just as a tree has many roots that help stabilize and nourish it, so too can you have many anchors that help stabilize you. By having multiple anchors, you distribute the strain of whatever life brings your way among those multiple anchors.

Once you have multiple ways to anchor your self-image and your center, you can begin to make decisions that people who are anchored in a single self-image could never consider. If you have seven well-integrated aspects of your self-image relying on seven different anchors, it's simple to pick up an anchor and re-evaluate it. You can consider whether the standard that you're using to determine whether you're a good dad or not is the right standard or even a reasonable standard. With multiple anchors, you suddenly can re-evaluate them one by one—making the way that you anchor your self-image, your identity, and your center dynamic.

Times change, people change, life changes. People with one anchor and only one aspect of their self-image intact can't take the risk of being adrift if they pick up an anchor to contemplate it. They're locked into whatever perspective they gained when they established the anchor (consciously or, more often, unconsciously). Being fixed in a spot while the world is changing isn't the best place to be.

Mindfulness

No discussion of how to build resilience would be complete without a discussion about mindfulness. However, mindfulness doesn't need to be a big thing that you can't get your arms around. Mindfulness is simply being aware: aware of yourself and aware of your environment. Awareness requires that you pay attention. You're not looking for threats; you're simply trying to be in the moment and process what you're experiencing.

There are meditative paths to mindfulness, but simply being quiet and shifting your focus from your body and what you're feeling to the environment and back again is enough. With practice, this conscious consideration of yourself and your world leads to a better unconscious awareness of yourself and how you respond to your environment. It's like riding a bike or driving a car. At first, it requires your entire attention. Over time, as you get more practice, it becomes easier to ride a bike or drive a car without thinking about it consciously at all.

Creating space in your world and using that space to just be, to sit and observe, leads to a self-awareness that makes you calmer in the face of threats and the thunder happening in the world around you.

Mindset

Throughout the book, we've been talking about how to change your mindset. It's more than just being aware of yourself and the environment around you: it's taking a different view of these things. Carol Dweck has researched the impact that a mindset can make and how to influence others' mindsets (Dweck 2006).

Dweck explains that we can either fall into a fixed mindset—that things are fixed and cannot change—or a growth mindset—that, fundamentally, we can grow and change. The first belief leads you to helplessness and burnout; the second belief leads you to hope and resilience. If there's nothing that you can do to change yourself or your circumstances, then learned helplessness and burnout should take over. If you know that, through hard work, you can change your circumstances, then you have every reason to persist even when the going gets tough. You never know how soon you'll be able to get past whatever barriers you're facing today, but you have the belief that you will get past them.

> If you know that, through hard work, you can change your circumstances, then you have every reason to persist even when the going gets tough.

Developing the growth mindset in ourselves and others is as simple as shifting from praising (or condemning) inherent qualities of a person and instead focusing on the work being done and how it leads to results. When viewing others, we consciously connect their work to the outcomes they see. When viewing ourselves, we attribute our success not to our genetics but to our grit.

Grit

Angela Duckworth argues that grit is passion and perseverance or, alternatively, self-discipline wedded to a dedicated pursuit of a goal (Duckworth 2016). We've tried to help you find your passion throughout the book, so we'll focus our discussion on perseverance. Perseverance is continuing even when things are hard. Some of this comes from the desire to reach the object of our passion, and some of it is residual perseverance from other things that we've pursued and achieved.

If we find that we're persistent in something and therefore get the results we want, we can praise ourselves for our perseverance. With repetition, this self-talk will develop more perseverance. We learn to consider whether we're giving up too early or if the success we desire is just around the corner.

Sometimes, after we've made our way through something with our grit, we do what Brené Brown calls "gold-plating grit." That is, we fail to acknowledge the struggle, the hurt, and the fear that are experienced while living out our grit (B. Brown 2015). If we want to continue to develop our persistence, and therefore grit, we must recognize the persistence we've shown and the hardships we've endured.

Developing persistence is a mental game in reminding ourselves that we can succeed in the long term. However, we can create situations that give us the opportunity to get continual feedback that we're learning and growing. When that happens, we may find ourselves in the psychological state of flow.

Flow

In one study, Mihaly Csikszentmihalyi paged beepers carried by study participants, and they scribbled notes about their thoughts and feelings. From the results, he realized that the more they were engaged with a task, the more likely it was that they were upbeat (Csikszentmihalyi 1990). Csikszentmihalyi followed this thread, which led to the concept of flow, a self-reinforcing state where challenge and skill are held in balance, and the outside world, including your sense of time, goes out of focus.

These experiences are described as substantially more productive (400 percent), intensely positive experiences. Learning how to get into flow, and stay in flow, can be a powerful way to fight off the attack of burnout. Even though flow can substantially increase your productivity, it doesn't necessarily change the pace at which you should attempt to make and sustain change.

CHAPTER SUMMARY

- We can resist burnout when we see it coming by increasing our personal agency. We do this through recognizing results, soliciting support, and having strong self-care.
- Understanding burnout helps to develop resilience, which helps to prevent burnout.
- Identifying your values and boundaries and being able to clearly articulate them is a key part of the process of finding your center or stable core.

- An integrated self-image includes recognizing the multiple aspects and roles you have.
- Multiple anchors and goals build resilience and support positive movement in some areas even when other areas are stuck.
- A mindset that supports the belief that we can grow and change rather believing things will never change builds resilience.
- Recognizing that you have persevered and had success builds resilience.

DISCUSSION QUESTIONS

1. Being able to articulate your beliefs and boundaries is important in finding your center core. What are ten core beliefs or boundaries you hold?

2. When you develop an understanding of your self-images, these will build multiple anchors and resiliency. What are at least five self-images you have?

3. Think about a few times when you have persevered through a difficult situation. What are some ways your determination (or grit) supported your success?

CHAPTER 17

Congruent Change

Resilience is about managing change. Some of that change is internally driven and desired. It's the change that you want to impart to the world. The other part of that change is what's happening in the world around you and how you respond to that change. In both kinds of change, there's a virtue of patience that must exist, whether that patience is for yourself or others.

Congruent change is about finding a pace of change that you and others can accept. Collectively, we need to find a pace of change that is fast enough to keep everyone seeing progress and simultaneously slow enough that it doesn't seem overwhelming. That starts with the right expectations about the changes we want to make.

MAKING CHANGE

If only *they* would change, it would make things better for *me*. We've all said some variation of this, either to ourselves or out loud. We want to change the people and the world around us in ways that fit our views. We all want to control, but none of us want to be controlled (J. Miller 1992). The problem with this is that others don't want to change. The world doesn't want to change. However, we believe that we have the power to change it in some ways.

It really doesn't matter whether the change that we intend is small or large. The tendency will be for things to stay as they are until some force acts on them in a way that compels or encourages them to change. We're seeking to be that force that encourages change, but how do we do that?

Hirschman's Hypothesis

Albert Hirschman was an economist whose work *Exit, Voice, and Loyalty* lays out a framework for how people can live in a world that is inconsistent with their views (Hirschman 1970). The world is bound to not match our point of view. The key question of character is what are we going to do about this mismatch. Margie Warrell, in *Find Your Courage,* says, "Ultimately, courage has little to do with heroic acts and everything to do with the choices you make moment by moment, day by day, right throughout the course of your life" (Warrell 2009). *Crucial Conversations* expresses the challenge of facing opposing opinions differently. It says that we have three options: avoid them, face them and handle it poorly, or face them and handle it well (Patterson et al. 2012). Hirschman provided a framework for those choices when it comes to how to change your situation.

Options for Change

Fundamentally, Hirschman saw two options for change. The first option, exit, has people leaving the relationship. This is "the easy way out," where the person seeks to find another, more suitable situation. This can—but often does not—cause organizations to realize that their numbers are dwindling and act to change the situation through internal motivation.

The second option, voice, has the person providing comments, criticisms, and feedback designed to cause the situation to change more directly. Voice is the hard road. It's a courageous choice to be willing to accept the consequences of the candid feedback—even if those consequences mean an exit that is initiated by the other side.

Having the courage to seek the change is—unfortunately—quite rare. Too often, the risks of changing companies, social groups, churches, or friendships is too high to contemplate. Whether it's through our own exit or having our voice, the risks are simply too much to bear. That's why, all too often, we find that Hirschman's other two options, which protect the status quo, are used.

Options for Status Quo

While there are good options for encouraging the change you want, there are two other options. The first is neglect, which is to ignore or deny your desires to change the situation. In this, you create great internal strife for yourself, as you're intentionally—though sometimes unconsciously—living a lie.

> The second strategy is persistence or perseverance. This is a key strategy for accepting that you can't make the change you want right now.

The second strategy that maintains the status quo is persistence or perseverance. This is a key strategy for accepting that you can't make the change you want right now. Sometimes the timing and conditions simply aren't conducive for change. So, in that way, persistence can be a valid and useful approach that allows you to bide your time until the conditions are conducive or even favorable to the type of change that you would like to see.

However, persistence comes with a high risk of burnout. You know that you want to see change, and, at the same time, you know that you're not making any changes. There's an awareness that you are not making progress at this moment, and you don't know when you will make progress.

Change Is Hard but Not Impossible

Changing the world to the way that you think it should be is hard. *Leading Successful Change* states, "Study after study, decade after decade, reports similar findings, namely that between 50% and 75% of change initiatives fail" (Shea and Solomon 2013). The statistics in *Influencer* aren't any better: "Our review of the past 30 years of change literature reveals that fewer than one in eight workplace change efforts produces anything other than cynicism" (Grenny et al. 2013). *Change or Die* reports a much scarier set of statistics, including that 90 percent of people don't change their lifestyle after a heart attack, and two-thirds of former inmates are rearrested within three years (Deutschman 2009).

Statistics like those are frustratingly depressing. There certainly are many change initiatives, on both a personal and an organizational level, that aren't successful. However, while not every change initiative succeeds, some do. Successful changes tend to take much longer than we would expect. Everett Rogers spent a lifetime studying the rate of adoption of innovations (Rogers 1962). Innovations are changes that are successful, and, while some come quickly, others take decades to take hold. Rogers identified a set of factors that influence the rate at which change occurs: relative advantage, compatibility, complexity, trialability, and observability. When the factors were aligned, Rogers saw faster diffusion of the innovation.

When we're trying to create change, we need to find a way to have a pace that works for us in terms of our personal expectations for efficacy but is also congruent with everyone else's capacity to accept the change.

ACCEPTING CHANGE

When we're trying to make a change, the challenge is finding out how slow we can go and still feel like we're making progress. A different problem occurs when the changes are coming at us from the outside. In this case, our goal is to slow them down to a pace that's acceptable to us. When we look at the problem from the perspective of how change affects us, we really understand why we need to mediate our need for progress with our desire to be compassionate to our fellow man.

When too much change is imposed on us, we can get burned out because we feel as if things will never stay the same long enough to get any traction. The changes that come at us from industry, organization, family, and social circles can leave us feeling like we don't have anything to steady us in the storm. The changes that are coming seem large and uncertain to us—however, they often appear bigger than they are.

Dying Industries

It was years ago now. There were stories about how all software development would be moving offshore and how developers in the United States wouldn't have jobs. The development that didn't move offshore would be done by business users with tools that naturally understood what they wanted and created solutions without the need to have developers at all. In the two decades since these prognostications were made, they've not come true. Sure, there is more offshore development than there was twenty years ago. Sure, the tooling is better, and business users can do more by themselves than they could twenty years ago. However, developers are still employed and in demand in the United States.

Publishing has been on a downward spiral for the last twenty-five years or so. Easier access to self-publishing and print-on-demand technologies have made it easier for anyone to get published—and many have. The average number of copies per book title have been steadily falling. There are a few outliers that outsell the average by a wide margin, but even the most optimistic of publishers admit that it's not the same business as a quarter century ago. It's increasingly more difficult to get people to read books.

Everyone wants a webpage or a snippet that they can consume in a moment or two. At the same time, they bemoan the loss of depth in the world where everything is reduced to smaller and smaller sound bites.

However, publishing is not dead. There are still companies that are making money. They still employ hundreds of thousands of people. Print, too, was supposed to be dead, and though electronic books outsell the printed ones, there are still printed books flying off the shelves.

The point of this is even though the industries are going through periods of rapid change and turmoil, they're not gone. It will be decades still before the death of publishers or the loss of software development jobs in the United States. Much of what was forecast for the next few years is still decades away.

WIII-FM

Everyone listens to one radio station. The radio station is WIII-FM. It's all me, all the time. The full name for the station is "What Is in It for Me?" It's what everyone wants to know when they are confronted with any change— no matter the size or the source. It's always analyzing whether the change is a threat to the individual.

For Rob, the prospect that his chosen profession of software development was going to evaporate was terrifying. His second career in publishing as an editor and author was being challenged at the same time. The question was how he would keep adding value and providing for his family. Over the last twenty-five years, he's continued to do software development and has hired software developers. He's amassed author credit on twenty-six books and editor credit on another hundred more. Despite the changes in the industry, he's done well.

Perspective

As you might expect, the key to accepting change is to put it in a proper perspective, both in terms of impact and in terms of timing. There's no doubt that there will be a time when transportation will be ruled by self-driving cars, automatic, Uber-like services, and electric cars. However, that doesn't mean that you must immediately be concerned as a gas station owner, a car dealership, or an insurance provider. You need to be aware that the change is coming, but the change will be slow and gradual over more than a decade or two.

If you feel like you can't meet your personal objectives because the industry is moving too swiftly, it could be that you're expecting that the change will happen quicker than it actually will. When we're going to be impacted by a change, it's natural for us to overestimate the threat that it means to us personally.

> When we're going to be impacted by a change, it's natural for us to overestimate the threat that it means to us personally.

If you're feeling a lack of personal efficacy because you feel like things are changing too quickly, it's possible that this is true. However, in most cases, it just feels like it's changing too quickly. Most industries move slower than we believe. Even technology has broad, sweeping arcs, where some of the technology in use fifty years ago is still in use today. If you don't believe us, look up RS-232. It was a recommended standard (RS) for serial communication back in 1960, but even some new network gear today has the humble serial port on it.

PATIENCE

Whether it's waiting for the changes that you're trying to make or accepting that some of the changes you believe are coming to you aren't really going to happen, patience is an important tool. Patience is easier said than done, but it's something that can be developed. Just ask the man with the marshmallow.

Mischel's Marshmallow

In a room at the day care associated with Stanford University, a man has marshmallows, and he's using them to test children. The task is simple. If the child will just wait until the researcher comes back, they'll get two marshmallows. The trick is that one marshmallow is already in the room with the child, waiting to be eaten. The test is a delayed gratification test. Which children can wait for two marshmallows? Which children won't be able to endure the torture? This is Walter Mischel's experiment that was eventually labeled the "marshmallow test" (Mischel 2014).

The interesting part isn't the kids trying to resist the temptation. The interesting part is the follow-up research where they revisited the children after the test was long since forgotten. The striking thing was that those students who were able to wait and get a double reward were being rewarded in life. By nearly every measure, they were better off than the children who opted for the immediate gratification.

> The ability to delay gratification is correlated with better life outcomes. Better yet, delayed gratification can be taught.

It turns out that the ability to delay gratification is correlated with better life outcomes. Better yet, delayed gratification can be taught. You can teach students techniques to treat the marshmallow as not real or techniques for self-distraction. The result is a greater tendency to delay gratification—and better outcomes in life.

If you're still scooping up the goodies and living up your life with little or no delayed gratification, there is hope for you to learn techniques that will give you the opportunity for twice as much tomorrow if you're willing to give up something today.

Compounding and Currents

Ultimately, patience creates opportunities that simply don't exist when you must live in the world of "right now." Interest compounds. It makes financial assets bigger—and financial deficits bigger, too. The more you can live in balance with the changes that are happening around you, the more you can avoid the potential issues with compounding.

When it comes to making changes, it's not wise to always fight the currents that drag change along, either fast or slow. It's much wiser to work with the currents of change to avoid exhaustion.

CHAPTER SUMMARY

- Being resilient requires that you are able to manage change.
- Congruent change occurs at a pace that is fast enough to see progress and slow enough to not be overwhelming.
- There are four options to consider when meeting resistance to the changes you attempt to make to align your world to your values: exit the situation, speak up to seek change, ignore your desire for change, or persevere while maintaining the status quo.

- Persevering in a situation where change is needed increases your risk for burnout.
- Change, even desired change, can be difficult. We all want to know how change will impact us personally.
- Having patience to wait for what you want can create unexpected opportunities.
- Working with the current of change rather than fighting it can help avoid exhaustion and build resilience.

DISCUSSION QUESTIONS

1. What changes are creating challenges in your world?
2. We discussed four options for change: exit the situation, work to change the situation, ignore your desire for change, or persevere in the situation. Considering each of the changes that create conflict in your world, what is the most effective response for you at this time?
3. In what areas do you need to develop patience with the changes in your world? What does that look like in the short and long term?

CHAPTER 18

The Role of Hope

There is nothing more powerful in the prevention of burnout than hope. For that matter, there's nothing more powerful in the world than hope. From the legend of Pandora's box to the placebo effect, hope has a power that all the world's evils can't conquer, a power that can reduce pain and cure diseases. Hope is simply the belief that things will get better in the future. Whether we believe that the change will come by our own hands or by the hands of someone else, hope is that sometimes frail yet persistent belief that things will get better. Understanding burnout helps to prevent you from becoming entangled in it; understanding hope can help you learn to live with more of it.

HOPE IS NOT AN EMOTION

If given a test, most folks would quickly draw a line connecting the word "hope" to the word "emotion." Hope often clearly feels like an emotion, but it is really a pattern of thinking. A pattern of thinking can either play a game of worst-case scenario, where everything remains the same or gets worse over time, or it can be more helpful, expecting that things will get better soon.

> Hope often clearly feels like an emotion, but it is really a pattern of thinking.

Some researchers believe that emotions are part of the brain's predictive capacity, so one might expect that hope is itself an emotion (Barrett 2017). However, hope is a process whereby we transform our predictions. Hope allows us to shape how those predictions are made and whether they lead to the belief that the outcomes will be worst case or best case.

Worst-Case Scenario

In the chapter on psychological self-care, we discussed how some people don't play the worst-case scenario game very fairly, and we talked about some ways to interrupt the game to play it differently. The worst-case scenario game is one that leads to a lack of hope. However, there is another game that we can play, best-case scenario, that leads to more hope and to less burnout.

Best-Case Scenario

Hope is sort of the opposite of the worst-case scenario game. Instead of believing that everything will go poorly, we believe that everything will go just right. You'll meet the man of your dreams, even though you spend all your free time binge-watching TV shows on Netflix. You'll definitely pick the winning lottery numbers, except you don't play the lottery. You'll get that amazing job that you've always wanted, except that you've not done the work to develop the skills that you need. Unchecked, the best-case scenario game can be nearly as bad as the worst-case scenario game.

As with the worst-case scenario game, the question to ask is, "Would that really happen?" Clearly, you're not going to meet someone if you're never in situations that allow that to happen, and winning the lottery does require that you actually play. Hope, in contrast to these games, is rooted in the reasonable but persistent belief that good things will happen. You will find a job you like that will allow you to develop the skills you'll need for your ultimate job. You'll save enough money to buy the car of your dreams or your first house. There will be things that get in your way, but the general trend line will keep going in the right direction.

Hope is a thinking process, and it works by thinking best-case scenario thoughts that are grounded in reality but ready to fly free.

THE MAKEUP OF HOPE

The thinking process of hope is one lens through which to view hope, but another way of thinking about it comes from C. R. Snyder. According to C. R. Snyder in *The Psychology of Hope*, hope is made up of two components: willpower and waypower (Snyder 1994). Both components are necessary for hope to stay alive. Willpower provides the energy, and waypower provides the way of channeling and leveraging that energy.

> Willpower provides the energy, and waypower provides the way of channeling and leveraging that energy.

Willpower

Willpower is a renewable and exhaustible resource. We can regain our will-power just as we can exhaust it. While willpower is often pursued from the point of view of our ability to control ourselves, it's equally the source of power that contributes to our hope.

Exhaustion and Replenishment

For many, the concept of willpower seems like a fixed quantity. Either you have it, or you don't. However, if we look more carefully, we'll see that, even in our own lives, we'll have willpower at some times and not at others. There are a variety of reasons why we may pass up our favorite dessert on Tuesday but on Thursday evening eat the whole pie.

Willpower is a capacity we have that is consumed as we use it. The more we fight in our day to keep from telling our boss or customers what we really think, the less we have when we get home and open the refrigerator. Though it is possible to increase your amount of willpower, it takes purpose-ful practice, not just long, strenuous days (Ericsson and Pool 2016). In the moment, if we've consumed our willpower, we may have nothing left to stop us from eating too much.

The other side is that our willpower will naturally recover. If we're resting—not exercising our willpower—it will naturally return. It will return at a much faster rate if we sleep or find an activity that's enjoyable but not strenuous. Our willpower springs up from our soul into the res-ervoir of our current life. We can overspend it and deplete the reservoir, or we can underspend it to ensure that we have a large capacity when we need it.

Low Willpower Living

Low-willpower living is intentionally creating a life that doesn't require large amounts of willpower for day-to-day functioning. It might seem that low-willpower living is a cop-out. It may seem like it's an excuse to not build willpower; however, nothing could be further from the truth. It turns out that low-willpower living gives us a longer time to recharge and leaves us with greater reserves to face those unexpected challenges.

Low-willpower living is also relative. Low willpower is about consuming very little of the willpower you have available. Low willpower is, therefore, relative to the amount of willpower that you have. The benefit of low-willpower living is that you get to experience what it's like to resist temptations and be successful. When you're already running up to your limit, you're bound to run out of willpower occasionally. When that happens, most of us would condemn or criticize ourselves for our lack of willpower—even if we know we shouldn't. Low-willpower living means you've always got the reserves you need to be successful when the big temptations do occur.

We build greater confidence in ourselves by being normally successful, and only occasionally succumbing to overwhelming needs for willpower.

HALT

The research shows that there are times when our willpower is naturally lower—including when you're hungry or tired (Baumeister and Tierney 2011). While working in a twelve-step program, the idea of HALT came up. HALT is an acronym for:

- Hungry
- Angry
- Lonely
- Tired

These are the warning signs for addicts—when they need to be very careful. The same list is one that we recommend to watch out for when trying to have important conversations with others. We can fall into a belief that we'll always fail at willpower if we measure ourselves against unrealistic goals. We should expect to falter if we're always running our willpower low and trying to operate when we're hungry, angry, lonely, or tired.

Waypower

MacGyver was a television show in the late eighties and early nineties in which the show's titular star was played by Richard Dean Anderson. He would solve seemingly impossible situations with a bit of ingenuity and his trusty Swiss Army knife. Some of the situations were contrived and the solutions impractical, but you couldn't help but believe that MacGyver could do anything if he had his knife. That's waypower—the ability to create solutions to reach a goal.

If willpower is the energy to get things done, waypower converts that energy into something real and tangible. It's the tools necessary—like a Swiss Army knife—to make things work. Where willpower constantly ebbs and flows and is difficult to increase in capacity, waypower can be generated.

Skills Development

Have you ever learned something and didn't think that you'd ever use it again, only to discover that it came in handy somewhere down the line? Your math teacher said you'd use algebra all the time, and you thought "Yeah right!" until you needed to square off a deck using the Pythagorean theorem or know how long it would take to get to grandma's house if you sped a bit. The sum total of the skills that we have is our waypower. The more skills we learn, the more waypower we have.

Some might argue that the skills aren't useful. They can't help us know how to reach our goals if we don't know how we'll use them—except they can. Steve Jobs is famous for dropping in on a calligraphy course in college and then taking his love for the topic into a flexible font system that drove the Macintosh. Jobs could not have known, when he dropped in on the class, that he needed to know about calligraphy to support the growth of a computer company that he hadn't imagined yet. The skills we learn don't have to be targeted to anything in particular to be useful. All that's needed is a bit of creativity.

Developing Creativity

The traditional thinking is that creativity is something special that only a few people have. However, Tom and David Kelley, in *Creative Confidence*, challenge this notion (Keller and Papasan 2013). They believe that we're all born creative, but we stop being creative because of fear and the possibility of ridicule. We believe that only creative companies like Pixar can come up with creative movies. However, Ed Catmull, Pixar's CEO, admits that "early on, all of our movies suck" (Catmull 2014). It's the creative process that includes the entire team, the transparency they share, and the desire for excellence that allows their creativity to show through their movies.

Developing creativity isn't some mystical art form. You can rediscover your creativity by simply trying things, by being courageous in the face of the fear that someone might not like what you're doing or proposing. As you take more risks with your creativity, you'll develop it further and be more able to call on it when needed.

When you couple a wide base of skills and the willingness to be creative with the way that you approach solving challenges, you'll be able to express more waypower in the pursuit of your dreams.

THE HOPE ANTIDOTE

In everyone's struggle with life, there will be setbacks. Goals that were once apparently close are now off in the distance or seemingly impossible. It's in those times that hope's power is truly felt. Hope allows us to accept today's struggles knowing that tomorrow may be different. Hope stops the downward thinking spiral and curves the output upward. In medical research studies, hope, in the form of the placebo effect, is as powerful as—or more powerful than—most drugs. The most difficult thing to do when studying new drugs is to isolate the placebo—or hope factor.

> In medical research studies, hope, in the form of the placebo effect, is as powerful as—or more powerful than—most drugs.

Placebos

We've been speaking as if placebos and hope are the same thing, so let's walk that out. A placebo is quite literally nothing that should help you. It's typically a small amount of sugar or something else that's neutral to what's being studied. The person selected for a study either gets that—with no value—or something that may hold the key to a cure.

The problem is that usually both groups will improve in this situation. When measured against baseline, both groups will get better. That doesn't make sense, except that both groups will feel like there is a chance for things to get better. They'll both be filled with hope that the new treatment works—and that they're getting the new treatment.

Mitigating Fear

The other impact of hope is that it pushes back fear. Hope says that failure isn't a foregone conclusion. It might happen—but success might happen, too. We'll spend the entire next chapter talking about how to manage the fear of failure.

CHAPTER SUMMARY

- Hope is a pattern of thinking based on reality that embraces the belief that things will improve.
- Hope requires two components: willpower (the energy to make something happen) and waypower (a way to channel the energy).
- Willpower is a limited resource that can be used and replenished. You can maintain your reserves by recognizing when your willpower is running low and employing methods to build it up.
- Willpower is reduced when we are hungry, angry, lonely, or tired.
- Waypower utilizes skills that we may develop before we ever have the need for them.
- Developing creativity by trying out new things without fear of criticism can help develop more waypower and new options in pursuing your dreams.
- Hope allows us to accept today's struggles knowing that tomorrow may be different.

DISCUSSION QUESTIONS

1. Hope is a key component of resiliency. List the areas in your life where you feel the greatest struggles. What ways do you hope those struggles will improve?
2. Consider areas where you feel your willpower is low; what about those things consumes your willpower? What helps your willpower recover?
3. Waypower is built on our skills and knowledge. What new skills could you develop that would increase your creativity and knowledge base? What steps do you need to take to accomplish this?

CHAPTER 19

Failure Is Not Final

Failure is a scary thing. It never feels good, and sometimes it can feel downright devastating. However, learning to respect and not fear failure is a critical skill for resilience in life—including avoiding burnout. In this chapter, we'll get clear on what failure is, understand how to separate the outcome and the person, and recognize the need for failure.

WHAT IS FAILURE?

Failure is simply not meeting the intended outcome. It's not complicated, but, as humans, we fear failure, and our fear of failure runs deep.

Falling Out

At the root of our fear of failure is our fear that we'll be unloved, unappreciated, and cast out of our community. In the past, getting cast out of a community was a death sentence. We survived because we stayed in groups. To be exiled meant that you lost the protection of others. But we need to back up a moment and realize that, despite the sense-making for our fears, they're still relatively unfounded.

First, we must recognize that most people aren't kicked out of society into the wilderness any longer. We've got a multitude of social programs and charitable organizations that are focused on helping ensure that no one is either proverbially or physically left out in the cold. While, historically, failing to perform might have occasionally resulted in exile, it's not like that today.

Our internal voices are rarely quieted with such reasons. Even if we're not exiled, our brains reason, we'll become unloved or even unlovable. Surely that's reason enough to be afraid. However, that presumes a performance-based love that only functions when we're able to do something for the other person.

Agape Love

Agape love is frequently associated with the love God has for man. This example of unconditional love transcends and continues regardless of the situation or circumstances; there is nothing we can do to cause agape love to increase or decrease. This is completely different from performance-based love, where love is given if you meet someone's ideal or standards. In performance-based love, love is given and withheld dependent on behaviors.

Most of us were exposed to some form of performance-based love in our lives. If we did well, if we succeeded, we were praised. When we failed, we felt unloved or ridiculed. It may have been our parents; it could have been a teacher or a coach. It really doesn't matter where we encountered the performance-based love, it has left a mark on most of us. We lost the understanding that all humans are valuable, that we have intrinsic worth beyond what we can do for others.

When we forget that all humans are valuable, we open the door to atrocities like genocide (Tavris and Aronson 2007). When we connect and love our fellow man with compassion, we retrain our brains to an *agape* love that doesn't require performance. When we do this for others, we make it easy to accept that, when we fail, we'll still be loved.

OBJECT AND PERSON

Failure is—again—not meeting the intended outcome. It's an objective fact about something but not about someone. We can say the project failed, but we cannot, in truth, say that a person is a failure. Failures are only about some situation or object. They're not about a person, yet, too frequently, we assign the failure to a person, whether ourselves or someone else. People may fail at something, but they're not failures. They may fail at many things, but they're still not a failure.

> People may fail at something, but they're not failures. They may fail at many things, but they're still not a failure.

Consider many famous people who failed and lost and then became great. Abraham Lincoln may be the best president the United States ever had, but he racked up a long list of failures before that. J. K. Rowling may have sold millions of Harry Potter books, but, before then, she was broke and wondered how to feed her child. There is a long list of famous and revered people whom others might have labeled as a failure at some point in their life. It serves as objective proof that people aren't failures.

When addressing failure, it's important to realize that there will be another at bat. In fact, even professional baseball players only hit the ball every one in three times they're at bat. If you wanted to count the number of times that they've swung their bat and missed the objective, the ratio would be even larger.

OUTCOMES ARE A FUNCTION OF ENVIRONMENT AND PERSON

When it comes to baseball, the deck is stacked against the batter. It's not just a few professional baseball players that are near the one-in-three batting average—it's all of them. In this situation, we recognize that batters can't get much better than this. We acknowledge that the environment they're in doesn't allow for a better outcome. However, despite the awareness that there are circumstances where a one-in-three average is good, we have higher expectations of ourselves.

We expect that we should succeed at the things we do, if not all the time then at least most of the time, right? We aren't willing to accept that sometimes it's difficult to be successful, and we're certainly not willing to accept that there are times when it's impossible to be successful.

> We must learn how to deal with and accept situations that will never have a successful outcome.

In the movie *Star Trek II: The Wrath of Khan,* we learn that Captain Kirk was the only person to pass the Kobayashi Maru test. This is important because the test measures how you'll respond to an impossible situation. It shouldn't be possible to pass the test. We learn, however, that Kirk reprogrammed the simulation to allow for a favorable outcome. (He cheated.) His response was that he didn't believe in impossible situations.

We don't have the luxury of reprogramming life to prevent impossible situations, so we must learn how to deal with and accept situations that will never have a successful outcome. What makes this difficult is when all our friends and acquaintances seem to be succeeding. They've got the new job. They're the modern-day Norman Rockwell painting in the flesh.

THE FACEBOOK EFFECT

In the chapter on our capacity for personal agency, we spoke about how Facebook is used as a highlight reel to showcase your successes. It doesn't include any of the times when you missed the catch or tripped, stumbled, or fell. It's all the good times and none of the bad times. For most people, they post their successes to Facebook and quietly sink into a corner when they're failing or fumbling. Rarely do they post during these times, except for the occasional repost of a funny cat or dog video. As a result, what people post on Facebook tends to look like a highlight reel that is all successes and no failures. It's all the good without all the bad.

The problem is that somehow, subconsciously, we believe this Facebook fiction. We believe that there are no failures in the lives of the people that we see. More than that, most of these Facebook friends aren't friends at all. They're people that we know and we're willing to see parts of their lives. We're not able to see the reality because the reality is that we never see or speak to some of our Facebook friends outside of Facebook.

You can't edit out failure. You can't skip it or ignore it because it's through our failures that we learn and grow.

FAILURE IS HOW WE LEARN

It's often said that Thomas Edison was such the optimist that when asked about his failures in making the lightbulb, he responded that he had only succeeded in finding ten thousand ways to not make a lightbulb. Edison's resolution is admirable. Most of us would be worn down by the number of unsuccessful attempts. However, for him, they were ten thousand opportunities to learn. Sometimes the learning is no more than "that didn't work." Other times, however, the experiments left him and his team with critical clues that led him closer to his success.

When the TOPGUN fighter school was established, it had a clear mission: give pilots opportunities to practice their dogfighting skills without the usual costs of failure. Sure, the pilots failed—or lost—their dogfights dozens of times, but they were able to do so in a way that kept them alive (Ericsson and Pool 2016). The learning they gained from their failures allowed them to become better pilots when engaged with the enemy.

FAILURE ISN'T (OFTEN) FATAL

There are some situations where failure is fatal. If you lose a dogfight with an enemy while at war, you may find the failure is fatal. However, in most circumstances, failures aren't fatal. They may sting. They may mean a financial loss. For the most part, however, they shouldn't mean that we're unable to try again.

When coming to accept failure as an option—because it almost always is, despite quotes to the contrary—we recognize that it's not the end of our world. We can fail to save a patient but still know that we did the best we could—or that we made a mistake—and that there's nothing that can be done now. Many times, our failures help us become the people we are and want to be.

CHAPTER SUMMARY

- Failure is simply not meeting an intended outcome.
- Failure happens in situations or with objects. People may fail, but they are not failures.
- Humans are worthy of love regardless of what they do or fail to do. *Agape* love helps us be compassionate with others and ourselves.
- Everyone encounters failures in their lives. Failures are opportunities to learn what does and doesn't work.
- Learning through failure enables us to be the people we are meant to be.

DISCUSSION QUESTIONS

1. *Agape* or unconditional love is not based on performance. Identify a few people who have loved you unconditionally. How does this type of love make failing less devastating?
2. List three situations where you believe you failed. For each of these situations, what are the things you learned from it, or how did you grow through the situation?
3. Identify one apparent failure, considering both the event and its outcomes. How did this "failure" help to make you the person you are today?

Stress Management

By now, you've probably heard that poor stress management can kill you. You've probably seen celebrities who have made poor decisions under stress. You're probably clear that stress isn't good for you. In truth, however, stress isn't all bad. The right kind of stress in the right amounts can be energizing.

In this chapter, we'll take a tour of how stress works, its relationship to burnout, and what you can do to manage it.

WHAT IS STRESS?

Stress is a perceived threat to the status quo. It doesn't have to be an actual threat, nor does it have to be a large threat. The key is how the person perceives it. Catch a glimpse out of the corner of your eye of a stick that looks vaguely like a snake, and you may find yourself in a stress response. Harmful or harmless only matters from your perspective.

Ultimately, stress comes down to your perception of your degree of control. If you perceive you have a high degree of control, then your stress level will be low. If you perceive that life happens to you and you have little or no control, you'll have a high level of stress because every little thing is a potential threat.

STRESS 101

Most folks have experienced stress, but few understand how the stress response works or why it's both helpful in the short-term sense and detrimental in the long term. Fundamentally, our stress response was designed while on the plains of Africa (Sapolsky 2004). The typical response pattern was simple: see a lion, have a stress response, run.

> The stress response shuts down long-term projects temporarily to divert every ounce of capability we have to responding immediately.

The stress response was an adaptation to provide more resources to be able to run from the lion. Our bodies have a variety of long-term projects going on all the time. Digestion converts food into glucose. Our reproductive systems prepare to make babies. Our immune system fortifies defenses. However, if we don't escape the immediate and pressing problem—like a lion—none of our long-term projects will matter. So the stress response shuts down long-term projects temporarily to divert every ounce of capability we have to responding immediately.

The problem is that doing this costs energy in the long run. It's great that we can get the energy that's normally used for digestion, but the costs to restart the digestion machine are more than the costs of keeping it running—that's why the body normally keeps it running. The stress response is sort of like a payday loan. You know the costs are going to be expensive, but you need the money now, and there's not another answer.

Long-Term Stress

In the short term, the trade-off between additional capacity to outrun the lion works. In the long term, not so much. Humans have the unique capacity to predict the future and revisit the past. We create stories about what has happened and what may happen. These stories can trigger the stress response. That's OK if you want to feel a bit of excitement as you watch the latest Hollywood blockbuster, but it's problematic when the story isn't a story but is instead a worry.

When you're worried about how your kids are doing, how you'll pay your mortgage next month, when you'll find the next job, or a thousand other worries that humans have developed, you're triggering a stress response even if you're not intending to. While a lion tends to be a short-term problem with a short-term response, how you're going to pay the mortgage is a long-term problem. The stress response was never designed to be left on for that long.

The problems with long-term stress are numerous. Physiological changes cause a reduction in immune response. It causes the hardening of arteries. It reduces your lifespan. Neurologically, it's linked to depression, poor pain management, and addiction (Sapolsky 2004). There is new research coming out all the time about how sustained long-term stress is bad for us, so we should avoid it.

Stress Response

The way that we respond to stress is shaped by three things. First, our genetics play a part in how we'll respond to stressors. Some people are more sensitive to stress, and others less so. Second, our experiences shape our responses. A famous Adverse Childhood Experiences (ACE) study showed that there were long-term effects based on stressful events as children, when we had little control (Felitti et al. 1998). We learn from our experiences, whether that learning is positive or negative. In the case of the ACE study, the children seemed to learn negative lessons from their experiences.

The final component of our stress response is our ability to interpret what is happening to us and tell a story that either calms us away from the stress response or makes a proverbial mountain out of a molehill. Much of what we've been doing through the book is working on how to understand and rewrite stories differently. While our skills at interpreting stress are only one component of how we respond to stress, it's a powerful component. Even folks with bad genetics and worse experiences can have a positive relationship to stress with the right skills.

STRESS AND BURNOUT

"Job stress alone does not cause burnout" is the conclusion reached in the article "The Relationship between Job Stress, Burnout and Clinical Depression" (Iacovides et al. 2003). Despite this conclusion in peer-reviewed journals, the dictionary definition of burnout still contains "physical or mental collapse caused by overwork or stress." As a result of this common definition indicating a relationship to stress, you'll find many articles and web pages that equate stress to burnout or list stress as a cause for burnout.

> Burnout is caused when the inefficient consumption of resources caused by stress reduces personal agency faster, leading to personal agency exhaustion.

Some of the earliest writings about burnout convey that the energy spent in stress is a cause of burnout, and they simultaneously acknowledge that it's the lack of remaining energy that is characteristic of burnout (Freudenberger and North 1985). It's not the stress that directly causes burnout; instead, burnout is caused when the inefficient consumption of resources caused by stress reduces personal agency faster, leading to personal agency exhaustion.

Because of the early references pairing stress and burnout, many authors—including the authors of dictionaries—have concluded that burnout is caused by stress. Certainly, stress is harmful and unhelpful, but it's not directly responsible for causing burnout. Even if it's an indirect cause, how do you better manage stress?

STRESS MANAGEMENT TECHNIQUES

Another way that stress and burnout are related is that the techniques that are used to help prevent burnout are the same techniques that help manage stress. In the chapters on physical and psychological self-care, we discussed several ways to improve your overall health, and these same techniques are useful when managing stress. We've also spoken of how to change your perspective. Changing your perspective on a stressor can reduce its influence or make it disappear entirely. There are, however, three key techniques that we've not covered that are uniquely positioned to help you manage stress better—without requiring that you change the stressor. They are laughter, nature, and meditation.

Laughter

It is said that laughter is the best medicine. There are numerous research articles that indicate benefits of laughter, including immune response (Berk et al. 2001). Stress has been shown to reduce immune response (Sapolsky 2004). Laughter reduces stress (Hurley, Dennett, and Adams 2011). Together, this leads to the conclusion that laughter not only improves immune response but also improves other health factors impaired by stress.

In the book *Inside Jokes,* it is hypothesized that evolution developed humor as an error-checking routine to keep in check the conclusion-leaping in the human brain (Hurley, Dennett, and Adams 2011). Our ability to simulate, to "mind read," and to leap to conclusions can be hugely helpful to us as humans, but it necessarily means that we'll not always be correct. Humor is our way of identifying a fault in the conclusions we reached so that we can, presumably, refine them in the future.

In dozens of other ways, medical research has indicated that there are several positive health responses to laughter. These result in improved health outcomes. Beyond the management of stress, laughter makes you healthier. So, if you want to reduce your stress, find ways to laugh it up. Rob, during a particularly stressful time of his life, literally took standup and improvisation comedy classes, which seemed to help reduce the sustained stress. (This wasn't intentional laughter management, it just happened this way.)

Nature

There is a lot of research worldwide evaluating the positive impact of nature on people. Links are being found between well-being and environmental factors. There is even some evidence that "green"—or natural—environments improve physical and mental health and well-being (MacKerron and Mourato 2013). As more and more of us are moving to urban environments, it is more difficult to find places where we can escape into nature without the impact of the sights and sounds of people.

Taking a leisurely forest walk can awaken all your senses. Unlike a walk in the city, these nature walks also decrease cortisol levels, sympathetic nerve activity, blood pressure, and heart rate (Williams 2017). Too often, we do not experience natural environments enough to realize how restored they can make us feel. This time in nature can also help us be healthier, more creative, more empathetic, and more apt to engage with the world and each other. Nature is, indeed, a great place to enjoy self-care. The biggest boosts to our health are found with a minimum of five hours a month spent in nature (Williams 2017).

The positive impact of natural settings (especially coastal environments) is greater than the difference experienced from being with a friend versus being alone and about the same as doing favored activities like singing and sports versus not doing those things (Williams 2017). Finding ways to enjoy nature can help reduce the negative effects of stress that can lead to burnout.

Meditation

There is a great deal of confusion about what meditation is because there are so many variations and so many different opinions about which way is the "right" way to meditate. However, meditation isn't something that can be done right or wrong, nor can someone be said to be "bad" at meditation if they don't receive the results they're looking for. Bronnie Ware recounts a story in *The Top Five Regrets of the Dying* about a patient who had practiced meditation for decades, yet, nearing her death, found it impossible to meditate (Ware 2011). Mark Epstein, in *Advice Not Given: A Guide to Getting Over Yourself,* comments, "I was struck by how each of my patients wanted to be meditating the 'right' way and how each of them considered their own way to be 'wrong'" (Epstein 2018).

There are no "right" ways to meditate. There are, however, two major approaches. The first approach is to focus our thoughts onto a single thing, whether that be an object, a feeling, or a process such as breathing. The other approach to meditation is to consciously try to be present in the moment. That is,

> The key to meditation is a nonreactive and nonjudgmental response when your mind wanders. Note that it's when, not if

try to be consciously aware of the things that are happening around you. In both approaches, the key is a nonreactive and nonjudgmental response when your mind wanders. Note that it's when, not if.

When your mind wanders, you simply guide it back to the intent of the meditation and move on. It's not that you're doing it wrong, badly, or not well enough. It's simply that having a mind wander from the focus of meditation happens to everyone who meditates.

We find that simple (and sometimes short) breath meditation can be helpful to reduce stress. When a friend was recently anxious and manic, the only way that we could get her to sleep without medication was to lead her through a simple breath meditation: paying attention to her breaths and counting them. It allowed her to reduce her stress enough that she could sleep for a little while. Falling asleep while meditating isn't a bad thing, by the way. When you awaken, you can simply return to meditating. You can view falling asleep as an indicator of success in reducing the stress in your life.

Meditation can be a powerful tool to help you manage your stress and to give yourself some perspective on life.

CHAPTER SUMMARY

- Stress is a perceived threat to the status quo. The perception of the stress relates to how significant we believe the threat to be.

- The physiological stress response is intended to react to short-term, immediate threats. Over time, we have incorporated long-term stressors into the response. This leads to multiple long-term health issues.
- Our personal stress response is shaped by genetics, our experiences, and how we interpret what is occurring.
- Stress reduces personal agency. Personal agency exhaustion can lead to burnout.
- Physical and psychological self-care and changes in perspective can reduce the influence of stressors.
- Laughter, enjoyment of nature, and meditation are useful in reducing the negative effects of stress that can lead to burnout.

DISCUSSION QUESTIONS

1. What are your top five stressors? As you think about them, consider your perception of control in each of them.
2. Think about the stories you tell yourself about your stressors. How might you change the story so that you are able to calm the fears related to the stressors? Practice this with new and old stressors.
3. We added laughing, experiencing nature, and meditating to the techniques useful in changing your perspective. Choose one of the three and give it a try. How do you feel after that experience?

CHAPTER 21

Perspective on Perspective

Our perspective is at least a little wrong. Our perspective of reality doesn't match reality; it approximates it. Our brains are constantly trying to reconfigure our perceptions of reality to match it. However, this process doesn't always work. There are times when our biases get in our way. We're more likely to accept arguments that agree with what we already believe. We'll discount things that don't fit our world view.

Imagine walking through a dark room guided only by your memory of it. You take a step forward and stub your toe into a coffee table that you forgot about. You had a very tangible and painful experience with how your perception (your memory of the room) didn't match reality (the actual placement of furniture). Because we rely on our perceptions to know where we're going, it's important to turn on the light as much as possible and align our perceptions with reality. That's what this chapter is about: getting our perceptions to align better with reality.

MULTIPLE PERSPECTIVES

Have you ever been reminiscing with friends or family about an event that has long since passed and found that different people remember it differently? One person remembers that you were in the station wagon, and another remembers that you were in the family's Chevy Impala. Which one is right? Without photographic evidence, it may be hard to prove one version of the story is right and the other is wrong. While this is a case of different memories, the same thing can happen when evaluating your current situation.

Teachers routinely question whether they're making a difference or not. Each year, a new group of students enter the classroom a few short months after the last group left, and it seems like they're back where they started. They'll teach the same material to these students as the last set and wonder if it's making a difference. Inside their own heads, teachers have to wonder if they're making a difference.

By the end of last year, the teacher could still see places where the kids needed to learn and grow. There were things that the kids just didn't get in the limited time that the teacher had them. They're off, and the teacher doesn't hear from them. All the teacher can go on is their own perception of the difference they made in the students' lives. It would be easy to accept that a teacher didn't believe they were making a difference—from their perspective. If they could listen into a party over the summer where the kids were talking to each other about how much they've learned and the new options that were available to them, they might be able to adjust their perspective to know the change that they had made in some of the children's lives.

> It's best to try to understand other people's perspectives.

The best way that we can get multiple perspectives isn't to look from multiple points of view for ourselves. Instead, it's best to try to understand other people's perspectives.

BLIND SPOTS

We've all got blind spots. Literally, we've got a blind spot in each eye where the optic nerve connects, and we can't see the back of our head—not without some help (Eagleman 2011). While it's possible with some mirrors to look at the back of your head, in most cases, it's easier and more practical to ask someone to see if you have anything on the back of your head.

In addition to our literal blind spots, we have figurative blind spots as well. These are places where we don't have any reality to ground our perceptions—or we just don't have a perception. These blind spots are surprisingly common and just as hidden from our view as our literal blind spots. The beauty of our human condition is that those around us don't have the same blind spots. We can put their perspective—their picture of the world— together with ours through our ability to communicate, and, collectively, we can minimize the impact that the blind spots have on us.

WHAT REALLY MATTERS?

We spent some time in a previous chapter discovering our goals and trying to understand what we were aiming for, but what we didn't address is whether our goals really matter in the end. We've had plenty of goals that we've missed. We've had plenty of goals that we've given up on because we've discovered they're not going to pan out. We've even got goals and initiatives that we're not making progress on as we wait for the right timing.

Take, for instance, our Kin-to-Kid Connection Child Safety Cards. They're designed to teach kids and their parents how to stay safe while giving them a structure to communicate. We originally developed them in 2015, but, to date, we've not really gained the distribution we want to get this critical information to parents and kids. We may have to give up on the cards at some point, or they may take off. It's easy to see how we might feel like we're unable to make progress on this project and how we might get burned out on it.

Sometimes, even though the goal is what we want, it doesn't mean that it's going to work out in our time or in our way. At those times, it's important to take a step back and evaluate what really matters.

Most of the goals that we set won't matter in one thousand years. Very few things that have ever been done have survived thousands of years. We could cite pyramids, Stonehenge, and Petra (the ancient site used as the holding place for the Holy Grail in *Indiana Jones and the Last Crusade*) as examples of things that have lasted a thousand years. However, the list of things that have survived that long is short.

Even if we shorten the time horizon to one hundred years, the number of goals we set that will matter is still pretty short. We could argue that helping our children might last one hundred years. But will the professional accomplishments be remembered that long? While, initially, this is a depressing thought, that there is very little we'll leave the world, it can be liberating, too.

Smaller Movements, Larger Goals

The liberation comes as we learn that we don't have to make big progress on any goal. It's quite enough to move a very large goal an infinitesimally small amount, even if that amount is imperceptible. When you give up the illusion that anyone has made a truly huge change in the world, you can focus on the things that you *can* do without concern for whether the change that you make is good enough.

> Liberation comes as we learn that we don't have to make big progress on any goal.

There's a story of two boys walking along a beach, where thousands of starfish are stranded on the sand. As they're walking, one of the boys continues to pick up starfish and throw them gently back into the water. The other boy asks in disbelief, "What are you doing? The few that you're throwing back can't matter." Quietly, the first boy picks up a starfish and tosses it back into the water before responding, "It mattered to that one." In the grand scheme of things, it can be that our actions aren't monumental. However, for those whose lives we touch, we can make a big difference.

It's About Others

If you're still struggling with your goals and feeling like you're not making a difference, it may be worth asking if the goals are about you—or about others.

CHAPTER SUMMARY

- Our perspective is simply our perspective. We try to make reality match our perspective, rather than the other way around.
- It is useful to look for physical evidence and others' input to evaluate how your perspective aligns with reality.
- It is important to consider what really matters when making and evaluating goals.
- The change you make may not be as large as you would like.
- The change you make for one person may change their entire world.

DISCUSSION QUESTIONS

1. Evaluate your perspective of progress, success, or impact related to a few of your goals. Try to get a clear sense of your perspective, then ask a trusted person that understands your goal for their thoughts on your progress, success, or impact. How similar or different are these two perspectives?
2. Think about your goals and how they impact individual people as well as society. The impact you have on one person can change the world for that person.

Detachment

One of the consequences of burnout is disengagement. That is, you withdraw from life. The flame of compassion for others flickers. Strangely, one of the most powerful ways to prevent or recover from burnout, detachment, seems similar. At first glance, the difference between a healthy dose of detachment and the plague of disengagement is difficult to see. Where detachment frees you from the prison of attachment, the withdrawal of disengagement separates you from humanity.

DISENGAGEMENT

Most people encounter disengagement from time to time in themselves and in those they know. Someone suddenly stops caring about their favorite car club. They stop attending the weekly bingo events at the American Legion. Their figurines sit on the shelf unadmired. They pull back from the things they enjoy and disengage with life.

> Disengagement is a sure sign that something is going critically wrong. It's no wonder that, when people disengage, they can often feel it happening.

There is a lack of care for the activity or group. More powerfully, there's an exhaustion that makes one decide that the energy it takes to be engaged is more trouble than it's worth. Disengagement is a sure sign that something is going critically wrong. It's no wonder that, when people disengage, they can often feel it happening, and mental health professionals go on full alert.

Disengagement is bad and a sign of impending issues like depression, but it's not the same thing as detachment.

ATTACHMENT AS SUFFERING

In the Western world, attachment is generally perceived as a good, positive, and necessary thing. Mental health professionals believe that having attachment is good. Children need to be attached to their parents (Ainsworth et al. 1978). However, the Eastern view of attachment is different. Buddhists believe that attachment keeps us in a cycle of reincarnation and prevents us from entering nirvana. They also believe that life is suffering, and therefore attachment keeps us in suffering. That philosophy has advantages, but it doesn't do much to make you feel good with day-to-day life.

More practically, our attachment is to temporary things. They're things that we will necessarily have to part with. If we are attached, then, when we must let go, there will be suffering. When we move from one home to the next—even to a bigger home—we experience suffering because of our attachment to our old home.

DEBTS

We're all familiar with the problems of having debts. You're bound to something until you can repay it. We make payments on our homes and our cars until we can pay them off because we need shelter and transportation to live. However, every month, the bill comes due, and we must make another payment to keep these things. We can—and often do—end up working for these things instead of for

> If we hold onto things that are past their time, these things prevent us from moving forward.

ourselves. Too many people can't take meaningful, if less paying, jobs because they wouldn't make enough to pay their debts, like their mortgage. Those people have become trapped by their stuff.

In a way, because what we can and can't do is dictated by our stuff, the stuff owns us. We have to work to earn the money to pay for our stuff and the things that take care of our stuff. Sometimes our stuff seems to set the rules by which we live; this can induce suffering by preventing us from doing what we want to do or what we believe we are called to do because we spend so much time working to afford the roof over our heads, food in our bellies, and gas in our vehicles. Attachment can be seen like debt in that it constrains what we're able to do. If we hold onto things that are past their time, these things prevent us from moving forward.

So detachment isn't about disengaging with humanity; it's about freeing ourselves from the burden of attachment to things and ideas.

IMPERMANENCE

Everything is temporary. That's a core message of Buddhism and a truism in life. Great pharaohs tried to preserve their place on this planet with monuments, but so many of them are lost. How many pyramids have been discovered whose owner can't be found? How many monuments are no longer with us or are barely surviving? There may be significant efforts to preserve them, but this is not a testimony to permanence or one person's ability to stand the test of time but rather the ability to glimpse into a long-forgotten time.

It's easy to become fatalistic and wonder why we should care if everything is temporary anyway. The answer changes what you do and how you look at it. Instead of seeking to acquire material things—which are impermanent—you shift to how you can move forward relationships and help your fellow man. Instead of being concerned with what we can do and demonstrate or what we can make and measure, the focus shifts to how to build up others and form deeper relationships. Things remain impermanent, but you're moving the general direction of humankind in a positive direction.

These, too, are impermanent and fleeting, but the trajectory that is created when we're all focused on building up others' lives helps us avoid burnout and creates a better society. The trajectory leads us right through compassion.

THE ROLE OF COMPASSION

The fact that compassion, or love, is so central to every major religion can't be an accident. The idea that we need to care for one another isn't an artifact of a bygone time. Nor is it a fancy idea to which people can aspire but still not experience. Compassion—for ourselves and others—is woven into the very fabric of our being. We see it in children before they reach their second birthday. It surfaces in computer simulations (Axelrod 1984). Quite simply, everywhere that you peel back humanity, you find compassion.

It's compassion that keeps us from converting detachment to disengagement. Our care for others, in the form of compassion, isn't minimized by detachment. With compassion, we don't desire to disengage. To do so would essentially be turning our back on our fellow man and the slings and arrows assaulting them.

ENGAGED DETACHMENT

The difference between the unhealthy disengagement and a healthy detachment is that detachment is an active process. It's not that you're no longer engaging with activities and people, it's that you're making a choice to be detached from the outcomes.

In the case of our bingo example, the disengaged person doesn't bother to go. The detached person goes for fun and doesn't worry about whether they win or not. The disengaged can't bring themselves to be present and engage with the other people. The detached person goes for the relationships and plays along as the numbers are called, marking their sheets without a care that they win or not.

Detachment isn't about not participating. Detached people are participating. Detached people just aren't wrapped up in the outcomes. They don't believe they can control the outcomes, and therefore they aren't worried about them.

> Detachment isn't about not participating. Detached people just aren't wrapped up in the outcomes.

YOU'RE NOT RESPONSIBLE FOR WHAT YOU CAN'T CONTROL

We all love to believe that we're in control. We think that we're in control of our lives, and we forget the times when our lives took a turn due to an unexpected illness or injury. We conveniently forget the time we spent looking for another job when we lost the previous one. We forget how hard dating was once we're married because we don't need to remember it any longer. In effect, we lie to ourselves that we always have had our life under our control. Circumstances don't matter, only our willpower, our skills, and our perseverance.

The problem is that we really control very little. We control our actions— or, at least, we mostly control our actions. Many of our actions are under autonomous control. Still more actions happen the moment after we're startled, angered, or hurt. So even our ability to control our actions is dubious. If we've tried meditation, we're well aware that we don't really control our conscious thoughts as much as we have the capacity to guide them.

When we're confronted with the question "Why try?" the answer is that, by trying—whether we have responsibility and control or not—we move the arc of humanity further in a positive direction.

CHAPTER SUMMARY

- Disengagement is a consequence of burnout.
- Detachment is different from disengagement; detachment frees us from the burden of attachment to things, ideas, and outcomes.

- Focusing on building relationships and helping to build others up creates a trajectory that helps us avoid burnout.
- Compassion moves us to want to help our fellow man. With compassion, you don't desire to disengage.
- Engaged detachment moves us to participate in life without being attached to the outcomes.
- We cannot be responsible for what we cannot control. There are few things we have true control of, but once we realize we cannot be responsible for the outcomes of these things, we can become detached and fully engaged.
- We are free to impact the world without the burden of responsibility for the parts of the world that refuse to be changed.

DISCUSSION QUESTIONS

1. What sort of material things are you working for (like a house, car, yacht, etc.)? Do these things bring you joy, or are they a burden?
2. Reviewing your multiple roles, what areas do you find that you do not have control over yet still feel responsible for? (An example might be what your friend says to your significant other about dinner.)
3. As you process the ideal of not being responsible for what you can't control, ponder the experience of not owning the outcomes of those things you can't control.

Keep the Conversation Going

We're humbled by your interest in our book and your desire to keep yourself out of burnout and help others recover from it. We would like to keep in touch with you. *Extinguish Burnout: A Practical Guide to Prevention and Recovery* has a companion web site—ExtinguishBurnout.com—where you'll find tools and resources to make the process of preventing or recovering from burnout easier. From burnout inventories you can take to worksheets you can use to work your way out of burnout, the web site is a way to extend the information you found in the book.

We'd also love for you to sign up for our newsletter, so we can share more about how to leverage others' success in extinguishing burnout from their organizations and lives. You can sign up at ExtinguishBurnout.com/ newsletter.

Glossary

Acedia—a "lack of care" for things one once cared for, or a general lack of drive

Agape—one of three Greek words for "love," indicating universal love or compassion

Altruism—the desire to relieve another person's suffering to the point of being willing to accept possible consequences in doing so

Autonomy—the ability to work on one's own without active direction from someone else

Boundaries—a marking of who a person is and is not, which defines what they choose to be responsible for and limits what they will do for other people

Bucket list—a list of things you want to do before you die

Classical conditioning—pairing an involuntary response with a specific stimulus, so when the stimulus appears, so does the response

Compartmentalization—a defense mechanism that allows us to separate conflicting ideas or beliefs, which can be used as a coping strategy to defer the processing of a situation until the situation is completed

Compassion—the ability to understand the experiences of another along with the desire to alleviate their suffering

Cortisol—a hormone released by the adrenal gland in response to stress

Defining boundary—a permanent boundary that defines one's personality, which, if crossed, would change who one is as a person

Detachment—the process of freeing oneself from the burden of attachment to things and ideas

Disengagement—the process of becoming disconnected from the people or activities one cares for

Empathy—the ability to understand the experiences of another

Engagement—the state of emotional involvement or interest

Eros—one of three Greek words for "love," indicating romantic or erotic love

Intimacy—a deep connection with another person, which can be physical, emotional, or intellectual

Operant conditioning—the training of voluntary behavior, such as rewarding desired behavior with a treat or using punishment for undesired behavior

Philos—one of three Greek words for "love," indicating brotherly love

Protective boundary—a boundary that is used temporarily to recuperate, recover, rejuvenate, or heal

Self-care—care of the self without medical or other professional consultation; things you do to yourself for yourself

Shared intention—a single, shared thought across multiple people

SMART—an acronym describing goals that are specific, measurable, achievable, realistic, and time-bound

Sympathy—caring for the experiences of another without needing to understand those experiences

Vulnerability—the state of being exposed to the possibility of being harmed, or showing one's weakness, that can, in turn, open doors to intimacy with others

Bibliography

Adams, Douglas. 1979. *The Hitchhiker's Guide to the Galaxy*. London: Pan Books.

Ainsworth, Mary D. S., Mary C. Blehar, Everett Waters, and Sally N. Wall. 1978. *Patterns of Attachment: A Psychological Study of the Strange Situation*. Hillsdale, NJ: Erlbaum.

American Psychiatric Association. 2013. *Diagnostic and Statistical Manual of Mental Disorders*. 5th ed. Arlington, VA: American Psychiatric Association.

AvailTek LLC. 2018. "Child Safety Cards." September 21. https://www. kin2kid.com.

Axelrod, Robert. 1984. *The Evolution of Cooperation: Revised Edition*. New York: Basic Books.

Barna Group. 2014. *Churchless: Understanding Today's Unchurched and How to Connect with Them*. Carol Stream, IL: Tyndale Momentum.

Barrett, Lisa Feldman. 2017. *How Emotions Are Made: The Secret Life of the Brain*. Boston: Mariner Books.

Baumeister, Roy F., and John Tierney. 2011. *Willpower: Rediscovering the Greatest Human Strength*. New York: Penguin.

Berk, Lee S., David L. Felten, Stanley A. Tan, Barry B. Bittman, and James Westengard. 2001. "Modulation of Neuroimmune Parameters During the Eustress of Humor-Associated Mirthful Laughter." *Alternative Therapies* 7 (2): 62-76.

Brown, Brené. 2015. *Rising Strong*. New York: Spiegel & Grau.

Brown, Stewart, and Christopher Vaughan. 2009. *Play: How it Shapes the Brain, Opens the Imagination, and Invigorates the Soul*. New York: Penguin.

Buber, Martin, and Ronald Gregor Smith. 1937. *I and Thou*. Edinburgh: T & T Clark.

Cacioppo, John T., and William Patrick. 2008. *Loneliness: Human Nature and the Need for Social Connection*. New York: W. W. Norton.

Caldji, Christian, Beth Tannenbaum, Shakti Sharma, Darlene Francis, Paul Plotsky, and Michael Meaney. 1998. "Maternal Care during Infancy Regulates the Development of Neural Systems Mediating the Expression of Fearfulness in the Rat." *Proceedings of the National Academy of Sciences of the United States of America* 95 (9): 5335–40.

Catmull, Ed. 2014. *Creativity, Inc.* New York: Random House.

Chomsky, Noam. 1959. "Reviewed Work: *Verbal Behavior* by B. F. Skinner." *Linguistic Society of America* 35 (1): 26–58.

Christensen, Clayton M., James Allworth, and Karen Dillon. 2012. *How Will You Measure Your Life?* New York: HarperCollins.

Clark, Charles, Linda Stutz, James Snyder, Christopher Parkin, and Robert Meek. 2001. "A Systematic Approach to Risk Stratification and Intervention within a Managed Care Environment Improves Diabetes Outcomes and Patient Satisfaction." *Diabetes Care* 24 (6): 1079–86.

Cloud, Henry, and John Townsend. 1992. *Boundaries: When to Say Yes, How to Say No*. Grand Rapids, MI: Zondervan.

Csikszentmihalyi, Mihaly. 1990. *Flow*. New York: HarperCollins.

———. 1997. *Finding Flow: The Psychology of Engagement with Everyday Life.* New York: Basic Books.

Darwin, Charles. 1859. *On the Origin of Species.* London: John Murray.

Deutschman, Alan. 2009. *Change or Die.* New York: HarperCollins.

Dickerson, John S. 2013. *The Great Evangelical Recession: 6 Factors That Will Crash the American Church and How to Prepare.* Grand Rapids, MI: Baker Books.

Duckworth, Angela. 2016. *Grit: The Power of Passion and Perseverance.* New York: Scribner.

Duhigg, Charles. 2012. *The Power of Habit.* New York: Random House.

Dunbar, Robin. 1993. "Co-Evolution of Neocortex Size, Group Size and Language in Humans." *Behavioral and Brain Sciences* 16: 681–735.

Dweck, Carol S. 2006. *Mindset: The New Psychology of Success.* New York: Random House.

Eagleman, David. 2011. *Incognito: The Secret Lives of the Brain.* New York: Pantheon Books.

Ebbinghaus, Hermann, and Henry Ruger. 1855. *Memory: A Contribution to Experimental Psychology.* New York: Teachers College.

Epstein, Mark. 2018. *Advice Not Given: A Guide for Getting Over Yourself.* New York: Penguin.

Ericsson, K. Anders, and Robert Pool. 2016. *Peak: Secrets from the New Science of Expertise.* New York: Houghton Mifflin Harcourt.

Federal Bureau of Investigation (FBI), United States. 2018. "2016 Crime Rate Table 1." September 7. https://ucr.fbi.gov/crime-in-the-u.s /2016/crime-in-the-u.s.-2016/tables/table-1.

Felitti, Vincent J., Robert F. Anda, Dale Nordenberg, David F. Williamson, Alison M. Spitz, Valerie Edwards, Mary P. Koss, and James S. Marks.

1998. "Relationship of Childhood Abuse and Household Dysfunction to Many of the Leading Causes of Death in Adults: The Adverse Childhood Experiences (ACE) Study." *American Journal of Preventative Medicine* 14 (4): 245–58.

Florida, Richard. 2011. *The Rise of the Creative Class: Revisited*. Philadelphia: Basic Books.

Frankl, Viktor E. 1959. *Man's Search for Meaning*. Boston: Beacon Press.

Freudenberger, Herbert, and Gail North. 1985. *Women's Burnout*. New York: Penguin.

Freudenberger, Herbert J., and Geraldine Richelson. 1981. *Burn-Out: The High Cost of High Achievement*. New York: Bantam.

Fukuyama, Francis. 1995. *Trust: Human Nature and the Reconstitution of Social Order*. New York: Simon and Schuster.

Gawande, Atul. 2014. *Being Mortal: Medicine and What Matters in the End*. New York: Henry Holt.

Giorgi, Fabio, Antonella Mattei, Ippolito Notarnicola, Christina Petrucci, and Loreto Lancia. 2018. "Can Sleep Quality and Burnout Affect the Job Performance of Shift-Work Nurses? A Hospital Cross-Sectional Study." *Journal of Advanced Nursing* 74: 698–708.

Gladwell, Malcolm. 2008. *Outliers: The Story of Success*. New York: Little, Brown.

Gordon, Thomas. 1970. *Parent Effectiveness Training: The Proven Program for Raising Responsible Children*. New York: Harmony Books.

Gottman, John. 2011. *The Science of Trust: Emotional Attunement for Couples*. New York: W. W. Norton.

Grant, Adam. 2016. *Originals: How Non-Conformists Move the World*. New York: Penguin.

Greenleaf, Robert K. 1977. *Servant Leadership: A Journey into the Nature of Legitimate Power & Greatness*. Manwah, NJ: Paulist Press.

Grenny, Joseph, David Maxfield, Kerry Patterson, Ron McMillan, and Al Switzler. 2013. *Influencer: The New Science of Leading Change*. 2nd ed. New York: McGraw-Hill.

Haidt, Jonathan. 2012. *The Righteous Mind: Why Good People Are Divided by Politics and Religion*. New York: Pantheon Books.

Hanson, Rick. 2013. *Hardwiring Happiness: The New Brain Science of Contentment, Calm, and Confidence*. New York: Harmony Books.

———. 2018. *Resilient: How to Grow an Unshakable Core of Calm, Strength, and Happiness*. New York: Harmony Books.

Hari, Johann. 2015. *Chasing the Scream: The First and Last Days of the War on Drugs*. New York: Bloomsbury.

Heath, Chip, and Dan Heath. 2007. *Made to Stick: Why Some Ideas Survive and Others Die*. New York: Random House.

———. 2010. *Switch: How to Change When Change Is Hard*. New York: Broadway Books.

Hirschman, Albert. 1970. *Exit, Voice, and Loyalty: Response to Decline in Firms, Organizations, and States*. Cambridge, MA: Harvard University Press.

Hurley, Matthew M., Daniel C. Dennett, and Reginald B. Adams. 2011. *Inside Jokes: Using Humor to Reverse-Engineer the Mind*. Cambridge, MA: MIT Press.

Iacovides, A, K. N. Fountoulakis, St. Kaprinis, and G. Kaprinis. 2003. "The relationship between Job Stress, Burnout and Clinical Depression." *Journal of Affective Disorders* 75: 209–21.

Isaacs, William. 1999. *Dialogue: The Art of Thinking Together*. New York: Currency.

Jones, Jeffrey M. 2013. "In U.S., 40% Get Less Than Recommended Amount of Sleep." December 19. https://news.gallup.com/poll/166553/less-recommended-amount-sleep.aspx.

Kahneman, Daniel. 2011. *Thinking, Fast and Slow*. New York: Farrar, Straus and Giroux.

Keller, Gary, and Jay Papasan. 2013. *The ONE Thing: The Surprisingly Simple Truth Behind Extraordinary Results*. Austin, TX: Bard Press.

Kis, Anna, Anna Hernádi, Bernadett Miklósi, Orsolya Kanizsár, and József Topál. 2017. "The Way Dogs (*Canis familiaris*) Look at Human Emotional Faces Is Modulated by Oxytocin: An Eye-Tracking Study." *Frontiers in Behavioral Neuroscience* 11 (Article 210).

Kotler, Steven. 2014. *The Rise of Superman: Decoding the Science of Ultimate Human Performance*. Amazon Publishing.

Kotler, Steven, and Jamie Wheal. 2017. *Stealing Fire: How Silicon Valley, Navy SEALs, and Maverick Scientists Are Revolutionizing the Way We Live and Work*. New York: HarperCollins.

Laughlin, H. P. 1970. *The Ego and Its Defenses*. New York: Jason Aronson.

Lazarus, Richard S. 1991. *Emotion and Adaptation*. New York: Oxford University Press.

Lewin, Kurt. 1936. *Principles of Topological Psychology*. New York: McGraw-Hill.

MacKerron, George, and Susana Mourato. 2013. "Happiness Is Greater in Natural Environments." *Global Environmental Change*: 992–1000.

Maslach, Christina. 2011. *Burnout: The Cost of Caring*. Los Altos, CA: Malor Books.

Maslach, Christina, and Michael P. Leiter. 1997. *The Truth about Burnout: How Organizations Cause Personal Stress and What to Do About It*. San Francisco, CA: Jossey-Bass Publishers.

Maughan, RJ. 2003. "Impact of Mild Dehydration on Wellness and Exercise Performance." *European Journal of Clinical Nutrition* 57 (S2): S19–S23.

Mauss, Iris B., Allison S. Troy, and Monique K. LeBourgeois. 2013. "Poorer Sleep Quality Is Associated with Lower Emotion-Regulation Ability in a Laboratory Paradigm." *Cognition and Emotion* 27 (3): 567–76.

McPherson, Miller, Lynn Smith-Lovin, and Matthew E. Brashears. 2006. "Social Isolation in America: Changes in Core Discussion Networks over Two Decades." *American Sociological Review* 71: 353–75.

Meier, J. D. 2010. *Getting Results the Agile Way*. Bellevue, WA: Innovation Playhouse.

Miller, J. Keith. 1992. *Compelled to Control: Recovering Intimacy in Broken Relationships*. Deerfield Beach, FL: Health Communications.

Miller, Paul E. 2009. *A Praying Life: Connecting with God in a Distracting World*. Carol Stream, IL: NavPress.

Miller, William R., and Stephen Rollnick. 2013. *Motivational Interviewing: Helping People Change*. New York: Guilford Press.

Mischel, Walter. 2014. *The Marshmallow Test*. New York: Little, Brown.

Nichols, Shaun, and Stephen P. Stitch. 2003. *Mindreading* . New York: Oxford University Press.

Norris, Kathleen. 2008. *Acedia & Me: A Marriage, Monks, and a Writer's Life*. New York: Riverhead Books.

Oxford Dictionaries, s.v. "barrier (n.)," accessed February 11, 2019, https://en.oxforddictionaries.com/definition/barrier.

Patterson, Kerry, Ron McMillan, Joseph Grenny, and Al Switzler. 2012. *Crucial Conversations: Tools for Talking When Stakes Are High*. 2nd ed. New York: McGraw-Hill.

Paul, Annie Murphy. 2004. *The Cult of Personality Testing: How Personality Tests Are Leading Us to Miseducate Our Children, Mismanage Our Companies, and Misunderstand Ourselves.* New York: Free Press.

Penedo, Frank J., and Jason R. Dahn. 2005. "Exercise and Well-Being: A Review of mental and Physical Health Benefits Associated with Physical Activity." *Current Opinion in Psychiatry* 18 (2): 189–93.

Perlo, J., B. Balik, S. Swensen , A. Kabocenell, J. Landsman, and D. Feeley. 2017. *IHI Framework for Improving Joy in Work.* Cambridge, MA: Institute for Healthcare Improvement.

Physicians Foundation. 2018. *2018 Survey of America's Physicians: Practice Patterns and Perspectives.* Dallas: Merritt Hawkins.

Pink, Daniel H. 2011. *Drive: The Surprising Truth about What Motivates Us.* New York: Riverhead Books.

Pinker, Steven. 2002. *The Blank Slate.* New York: Penguin.

Popkin, Barry M., Kristen E. D'Anci, and Irwin H. Rosenberg. 2010. "Water, Hydration, and Health." *Nutrition Reviews* 68 (8): 439–58.

Pozen, Robert C. 2012. *Extreme Productivity.* New York: HarperCollins.

Pressman, Sarah D., Brooke N. Jenkins, and Judith T. Moskowitz. 2019. "Positive Affect and Health: What Do We Know and Where Next Should We Go?" *The Annual Review of Psychology* 70: 627–50.

Putnam, Robert D. 2000. *Bowling Alone: The Collapse and Revival of American Community.* New York: Simon & Schuster.

Rath, Tom. 2007. *Strengths Finder 2.0.* New York: Gallup Press.

Richo, David. 2010. *How to Be an Adult in Relationships: The Five Keys to Mindful Loving.* Boston: Shambhala.

Riso, Don Richard, and Russ Hudson. 1996. *Personality Types: Using the Enneagram for Self-Discovery.* Boston: Houghton Mifflin.

Rogers, Everett. 1962. *Diffusion of Innovations*. New York: Free Press.

Rosenzweig, Phil. 2007. *The Halo Effect: … and the Eight Other Business Delusions That Deceive Managers*. New York: Free Press.

Sapolsky, Robert M. 2004. *Why Zebras Don't Get Ulcers*. 3rd ed. New York: Henry Holt.

Scharmer, C. Otto. 2009. *Theory U: Leading from the Future as It Emerges*. San Francisco, CA: Berrett-Koehler.

Seligman, Martin E. P., and Steven F. Maier. 1976. "Learned Helplessness: Theory and Evidence." *Journal of Experimental Psychology* 105 (1): 3–46.

Shea, Gregory, and Cassie Solomon. 2013. *Leading Successful Change: 8 Keys to Making Change Work*. Philadelphia: Wharton Press.

Sinek, Simon. 2009. *Start with Why: How Great Leaders Inspire Everyone to Take Action*. New York: Penguin.

Smith, Warren Cole. 2017. "A Promise Kept: The Legacy of Robertson McQuilkin." June. http://www.breakpoint.org/2017/06/a-promise -kept/.

Snyder, C. R. 1994. *The Psychology of Hope: You Can Get Here from There*. New York: Free Press.

Spock, Benjamin. 1946. *The Commonsense Book of Baby and Child Care*. New York: Duell, Sloan and Pearce.

Stepper, John. 2015. *Working Out Loud: For a Better Career and Life*. New York: Ikigai Press.

Tavris, Caroll, and Elliot Aronson. 2007. *Mistakes Were Made (But Not by Me): Why We Justify Foolish Beliefs, Bad Decisions, and Hurtful Actions*. Boston: Mariner Books.

Tough, Paul. 2012. *How Children Succeed: Grit, Curiosity, and the Hidden Power of Character*. New York: Houghton Mifflin Harcourt.

Townsend, John. 2011. *Beyond Boundaries: Learning to Trust Again in Relationships*. Grand Rapids, MI: Zondervan.

Turkle, Sherry. 2011. *Alone Together: Why We Expect More from Technology and Less from Each Other*. New York: Basic Books.

US Department of Health and Human Services, National Institutes of Health. 2011. "Your Guide to Healthy Sleep." August. https://www.nhlbi.nih.gov/files/docs/public/sleep/healthy_sleep.pdf.

Van Zundert, Rinka M. P., Eeske van Roekel, Rutger C. M. E. Engels, and Ron H. J. Scholte. 2015. "Reciprocal Associations Between Adolescents' Night-Time Sleep and Daytime Affect and the Role of Gender and Depressive Symptoms." *Journal of Youth Adolescence* 44: 556–69.

Ware, Bronnie. 2012. *The Top Five Regrets of the Dying: A Life Transformed by the Dearly Departing*. New York: Hay House.

Warrell, Margie. 2009. *Find Your Courage: 12 Acts for Becoming Fearless at Work and in Life*. New York: McGraw-Hill.

Williams, Florence. 2017. *The Nature Fix: Why Nature Makes Us Happier, Healthier, and More Creative*. New York: W. W. Norton.

Wilson, Timothy D. 2011. *Redirect: The Surprising New Science of Psychological Change*. New York: Little, Brown.

Wood, Charles. 2013. "Development and Programming of the Hypothalamus-Pituitary-Adrenal Axis." *Clinical Obstetrics and Gynecology* 56 (3): 610–21.

Zachary, Vlad. 2015. *The Excellence Habit: How Small Changes in Our Mindset Can Make a Big Difference In Our Lives; For All Who Feel Stuck*. Evanston, IL: Central Street Publications.

Index

About the Authors

Robert Bogue has a driving passion for delivering solutions through both teaching and learning. His drive for resolving problems is fueled by his creativity and innovation—by his ability to find solutions that others cannot find. A business owner and community leader for over ten years, he has authored twenty-six books and edited over one hundred additional books. He knows how to ignite engagement, stop from burning out, and freeze a snowballing conflict in its tracks.

Robert is an engaging presenter who speaks at local, regional, national, and international events. As a fifteen-time Microsoft MVP and recovering technologist, he has spoken to tens of thousands of professionals in a wide range of audiences. Professionally taught as a comedian, Robert joins his ability to focus others with just a little bit of humor to create a wonderful experience for his audiences. He is committed to making the complicated simple with a flair that is both engaging and inspiring.

Contact Robert at Rob.Bogue@ThorProjects.com.

Terri Bogue has a passion for helping people be healthy and happy both physically and emotionally. As a clinical nurse specialist with over thirty years of experience in nursing, she understands how difficult health-care and life are for patients and providers. Through this experience, she has developed tools that support healthcare providers in delivering effective and compassionate care to their patients and themselves and reducing healthcare-associated infections.

As an author, Terri engages and encourages her audiences and has spoken at local, regional, and national events. She inspires people to learn what boundaries are and how to maintain them (both professionally and personally), cool down a conflict during heated situations, and prevent and recover from burnout.

When she is not working, she spends her leisure time dissolving conflicts and improving communication patterns in her own home among her seven children and enjoying moments of peace and quiet with her husband, Rob.

Contact Terri at Terri.Bogue@ThorProjects.com.